Prisons

Other Books in the Current Controversies Series:

Prisons

Bryan J. Grapes, *Book Editor*

David Bender, *Publisher*
Bruno Leone, *Executive Editor*

Bonnie Szumski, *Editorial Director*
David M. Haugen, *Managing Editor*

CURRENT CONTROVERSIES

Cover photo: Nancy A. Santullo/The Stock Market

Library of Congress Cataloging-in-Publication Data

Prisons / Bryan J. Grapes, book editor.
        p. cm. — (Current controversies)
    Includes bibliographical references and index.
    ISBN 0-7377-0147-1 (lib. bdg. : alk. paper). — ISBN 0-7377-0146-3
(pbk. : alk. paper)
    1. Prisons—United States. 2. Imprisonment—United States.
3. Punishment—United States. 4. Prisoners—United States. 5. Convict
labor—United States. I. Grapes, Bryan J. (1970–   ). II. Series.
HV9471.P782   2000
365'.973—dc21   99-41272
                                                                                      CIP

©2000 by Greenhaven Press, Inc., PO Box 289009, San Diego, CA 92198-9009
Printed in the U.S.A.

Contents

Chapter 1: Are Prisons Effective?

Yes: Prisons Are an Effective Solution to Crime

No: Prisons Are Not an Effective Solution to Crime

Chapter 2: How Should Prisons Treat Inmates?

system does not foster rehabilitation, many of these inmates are released only to return to a life of addiction and crime. With proper treatment, many of these inmates could break the destructive cycle of addiction and become productive members of society.

The standard of living for a convicted criminal living in prison is almost triple that of the working poor. While serving their sentences, murderers, rapists, and thieves enjoy state-of-the-art basketball courts, libraries, and cable television—luxuries that are beyond the reach of many hardworking Americans. To correct this injustice, the prison system needs to adopt a minimum standard of living for prisoners that is equivalent to the poverty threshold.

By allowing convicted criminals access to weight training equipment, prison officials are transforming convicts into stronger, more violent criminals. In addition to dramatically increasing an inmate's physical strength, weights pose a danger because they may be used as weapons. Inmate recreation programs should focus on less threatening types of exercise, such as calisthenics, aerobics, and basketball.

Weight training is a constructive way for inmates to channel their aggressive feelings and relieve the pressures of incarceration. Many prison officials note that inmates who lift weights have more discipline and self-esteem than inmates who do not train with weights. As a result, inmates who lift weights are less likely to engage in violent behavior.

Research has shown that isolating prisoners for prolonged periods of time is counterproductive as a safety measure. The extreme isolation and other harsh conditions encountered by inmates who are placed in supermax prisons often exacerbate antisocial tendencies. Most inmates who are placed in supermax facilities will eventually be released—either back into the general prison population or into society—and their experiences in supermax prisons greatly increase the chances that they will commit future acts of violence.

Chapter 3: Should Prisons Be Privatized?

Yes: The Prison System Would Benefit from Privatization

There is no potential problem with private prisons that is not matched by a similar problem among prisons that are run by the government. While privatization raises no new difficulties for prisons, it does offer many solutions to problems such as overcrowding, escalating prison costs, and time-consuming government bureaucracy.

highly controversial. Opponents of prison labor contend that prison laborers take jobs away from law-abiding citizens, and that prison-made goods unfairly compete with products made by free labor.

Yes: Prisons Should Use Inmate Labor

No: Prisons Should Not Use Inmate Labor

prisoners. If prison labor is allowed to expand, the jobs of many more Americans could be at risk.

Prison Labor Is Slave Labor *by John L. Zalusky*

The prison labor programs advocated by some politicians will create a slave workforce. Contracting inmates to private-sector employers who provide low wages—or no wages at all—is a morally reprehensible practice, and it poses a threat to businesses that pay workers free-market wages.

Prison Labor May Pose a Threat to Public Safety
by Christine Long-Wagner

Rather than helping to rehabilitate prisoners, some prison jobs are exacerbating criminal behavior. Some prisons offer inmates positions in airline reservations, telemarketing, and fundraising. The inmates who fill these positions have access to such personal information as credit card numbers, addresses, and phone numbers, and in many cases inmates have used this information to commit crimes upon their release.

Foreword

By definition, controversies are "discussions of questions in which opposing opinions clash" (Webster's Twentieth Century Dictionary Unabridged). Few would deny that controversies are a pervasive part of the human condition and exist on virtually every level of human enterprise. Controversies transpire between individuals and among groups, within nations and between nations. Controversies supply the grist necessary for progress by providing challenges and challengers to the status quo. They also create atmospheres where strife and warfare can flourish. A world without controversies would be a peaceful world; but it also would be, by and large, static and prosaic.

The Series' Purpose

The purpose of the Current Controversies series is to explore many of the social, political, and economic controversies dominating the national and international scenes today. Titles selected for inclusion in the series are highly focused and specific. For example, from the larger category of criminal justice, Current Controversies deals with specific topics such as police brutality, gun control, white collar crime, and others. The debates in Current Controversies also are presented in a useful, timeless fashion. Articles and book excerpts included in each title are selected if they contribute valuable, long-range ideas to the overall debate. And wherever possible, current information is enhanced with historical documents and other relevant materials. Thus, while individual titles are current in focus, every effort is made to ensure that they will not become quickly outdated. Books in the Current Controversies series will remain important resources for librarians, teachers, and students for many years.

In addition to keeping the titles focused and specific, great care is taken in the editorial format of each book in the series. Book introductions and chapter prefaces are offered to provide background material for readers. Chapters are organized around several key questions that are answered with diverse opinions representing all points on the political spectrum. Materials in each chapter include opinions in which authors clearly disagree as well as alternative opinions in which authors may agree on a broader issue but disagree on the possible solutions. In this way, the content of each volume in Current Controversies mirrors the mosaic of opinions encountered in society. Readers will quickly realize that there are many viable answers to these complex issues. By questioning each author's conclusions, students and casual readers can begin to develop the critical thinking skills so important to evaluating opinionated material.

Current Controversies is also ideal for controlled research. Each anthology in the series is composed of primary sources taken from a wide gamut of informational categories including periodicals, newspapers, books, United States and foreign government documents, and the publications of private and public organizations. Readers will find factual support for reports, debates, and research papers covering all areas of important issues. In addition, an annotated table of contents, an index, a book and periodical bibliography, and a list of organizations to contact are included in each book to expedite further research.

Perhaps more than ever before in history, people are confronted with diverse and contradictory information. During the Persian Gulf War, for example, the public was not only treated to minute-to-minute coverage of the war, it was also inundated with critiques of the coverage and countless analyses of the factors motivating U.S. involvement. Being able to sort through the plethora of opinions accompanying today's major issues, and to draw one's own conclusions, can be a complicated and frustrating struggle. It is the editors' hope that Current Controversies will help readers with this struggle.

Greenhaven Press anthologies primarily consist of previously published material taken from a variety of sources, including periodicals, books, scholarly journals, newspapers, government documents, and position papers from private and public organizations. These original sources are often edited for length and to ensure their accessibility for a young adult audience. The anthology editors also change the original titles of these works in order to clearly present the main thesis of each viewpoint and to explicitly indicate the opinion presented in the viewpoint. These alterations are made in consideration of both the reading and comprehension levels of a young adult audience. Every effort is made to ensure that Greenhaven Press accurately reflects the original intent of the authors included in this anthology.

"According to the U.S. Department of Justice, if the United States continues to incarcerate its citizens at the current rate, one in every 20 Americans born in 1997 can expect to spend some time behind prison walls."

Introduction

In 1971 there were fewer than 200,000 inmates serving time in America's state and federal prisons. During the 1980s and early 1990s, the American public's fear of rising violent crime—mainly attributable to the explosion of the crack cocaine trade in the 1980s—inspired many politicians to pass laws that imposed harsher sentences on those who engaged in criminal behavior. "Three strikes" laws, which mandate an automatic life sentence for a third felony conviction, and "truth-in-sentencing" laws, which require violent criminals to serve at least 85 percent of their sentences, combined with America's "War on Drugs" to fuel a prison population increase of unprecedented proportions. As of 1996, there were more than 1.7 million people behind bars in the United States. California alone has more prisoners than France, Great Britain, Germany, Japan, Singapore, and the Netherlands combined.

Since the 1970s, over 1,000 new prisons and jails have been constructed to accommodate the massive influx of inmates, and more facilities are needed to relieve the dangerously overcrowded conditions found in most prisons. The cost of convicting, housing, and feeding America's prisoners now exceeds 120 billion dollars per year. Three states—New York, California and Texas—spend more on incarcerating criminals than on higher education. Because prison construction and maintenance are consuming more from limited government budgets, many social critics are reexamining the effectiveness of increased incarceration as a solution to crime.

Advocates of the get-tough approach to crime argue that the benefits of increased incarceration far outweigh the budgetary difficulties associated with prison expansion. According to Steven D. Levitt, a member of the Harvard Society of Fellows, each criminal taken off the streets eliminates between two and three violent crimes a year, and over ten property crimes. Moreover, Levitt contends, the monetary cost of crime is greater than the cost of incarceration. "The economic benefits alone of preventing those crimes amount to approximately $45,000—well above annual incarceration costs that average $25,000 to $35,000 per prisoner," declares Levitt.

Furthermore, many critics contend that the increase in incarceration has had a pronounced impact on crime rates. According to 1998 FBI statistics, the overall

13

rate of serious crime is at a 25-year low. Pete du Pont, policy chairman of the National Center for Policy Analysis (NCPA), credits the increase in imprisonment with the drop in crime. According to du Pont, harsher sentencing guidelines serve as a deterrent to would-be criminals. "A major reason for the one-third crime slide in the 1990s is that crime has become expensive for adult perpetrators. The likelihood of serving prison time for committing a serious violent crime or a burglary has increased substantially," du Pont maintains.

Supporters of the get-tough approach to crime believe that society must build more prisons and incarcerate greater numbers of criminals, regardless of the cost, if any further drop in the crime rate is to be made. Rabbi Stephen Fuchs argues that society's safety is more important than the extra money it would take to keep more criminals in prison for longer periods of time. "To keep violent offenders locked up, society must embark on a massive program to build more prisons. We must, though, be willing to raise the necessary tax dollars. I, for one, am willing to pay the price. Violent felons should never be released for lack of prison space in which to keep them," says Fuchs.

Opponents of prison expansion, however, argue that America's policy of incarceration has been a costly failure. Critics of the prison system contend that incarceration is counterproductive in fighting crime because prisons exacerbate criminal behavior rather than deter it. According to Robert W. Winslow, "The nationwide recidivism . . . rate for prison inmates is 70 percent, and graduates of our prison system usually progress toward more serious crimes. This is because prison inmates must learn and adhere to an 'inmate code' to survive. This code emphasizes racism, retaliatory violence and predatory attitudes regarding sex and property."

Other critics of prison expansion argue that increased incarceration has relatively little effect on overall crime rates. According to the National Criminal Justice Commission (NCJC), the majority of the prison population are low-level drug dealers. These low-level dealers are easily replaceable because the drug trade is fueled by demand. When one dealer is arrested and convicted, another always steps forward to take his or her place. The NCJC argues that "by the time the criminal justice system has passed through several generations of drug dealers, billions of dollars have been spent and the corner is still scattered with empty vials of crack."

According to the U.S. Department of Justice, if the United States continues to incarcerate its citizens at the current rate, one in every 20 Americans born in 1997 can expect to spend some time behind prison walls. Some critics maintain that this statistic is indicative of the failure of America's prison policy. Opponents of prison expansion argue that the money allocated for prisons would be better spent on education and preventive programs. Gil Kerlikowske, police commissioner of Buffalo, New York, attests that "we'll win the war on crime when we invest tax dollars in America's most vulnerable kids, instead of waiting until they become America's most wanted adults." In addition to investing in preventive measures, many critics insist that a significant portion of the inmate population would benefit more from intensively supervised probation and drug treatment than serving expensive prison sentences. Supporters of prison expansion, however, maintain that America's high rate of incarceration is not so much an indication of a failed prison policy as it is an indication of the level of lawlessness in the United States. Economist and legal scholar Michael K. Block declares, "There are too many prisoners because there are too many criminals committing too many crimes." *Prisons: Current Controversies* offers a variety of perspectives on the prison system and its role in American society.

Chapter 1

Are Prisons Effective?

Chapter Preface

According to a 1998 report by the Bureau of Justice Statistics, there are more than 1.7 million people behind bars in America. To keep up with the rapidly rising prison population, state and federal governments have embarked on a prison-building spree of unprecedented proportions, committing close to $120 billion dollars to convict and house criminals. Despite the dramatic increase in prison building, however, American prisons remain dangerously overcrowded.

According to many experts, America's overflowing prisons are symptomatic of a failed corrections system. Monsignor William B. O'Brien, president and cofounder of the Daytop Village drug treatment program, contends that a large percentage of the inmates clogging the prison system are nonviolent drug offenders that pose relatively little threat to society. O'Brien maintains that sending drug addicts to prison is ultimately counterproductive. "For . . . years we've been filling our prisons with vulnerable, low-level addicts. By doing so, we've treated them to a university course in crime, so that when they're finally released, they hit the streets as new members of the crime network. We've positioned them to be accomplished criminals." According to O'Brien, as much as eighty percent of the prison population would benefit more from intensive drug treatment programs than incarceration.

Proponents of a get-tough approach to crime, however, contend that the majority of inmates in America's prisons are not harmless drug addicts, but dangerous criminals with violent histories who pose a serious threat to the public. Richard K. Willard, former assistant attorney general, argues that "many a putative first offender actually has a lengthy record of prior criminal conduct as a juvenile." Since juvenile records are sealed or expunged, Willard contends, the criminal histories of many seemingly harmless drug offenders remain secret—even if they have committed serious violent crimes. "It is quite predictable that most of those convicts will commit violent and predatory crimes as soon as they are released," Willard says. In Willard's view, prison overcrowding can only be remedied by building more prisons to incapacitate as many criminals as possible.

Whether the prison system is a proper and effective way to prevent crime is the question debated in the following chapter.

The Prison System Works

by Andrew Peyton Thomas

About the author: *Andrew Peyton Thomas is an attorney in Phoenix, Arizona. He is the author of* Crime and the Sacking of America: The Roots of Chaos.

Fox Butterfield of the *New York Times* regularly reports on what he sees as one of the great anomalies of the age: Incarceration rates are rising while crime rates are falling. An August 1998 article titled "Prison Population Growing Although Crime Rate Drops" was typical. Butterfield began, "The nation's prison population grew by 5.2 percent in 1997, according to the Justice Department, even though crime has been declining for six straight years, suggesting that the imprisonment boom has developed a built-in growth dynamic independent of the crime rate, experts say."

By "experts say," Butterfield meant that many liberal criminologists agree with him. To him and his likeminded profs, the continued rise in incarceration rates during a time of declining crime rates is a mystery tinged with injustice. As Butterfield stated in a January 1998 article, the rise in incarceration rates is prompting "troublesome questions" about "whether the United States is relying too heavily on prison sentences to combat drugs and whether the prison boom has become self-perpetuating."

Yet Butterfield's own article in August 1998 had an answer to these questions. He noted that 52 percent of the total increase in male prisoners in 1997 came from criminals convicted of violent offenses. Only anarchists would pronounce this a tragedy.

Locking Up the Right People

As for drug offenses, the vast majority of inmates are career criminals, as demonstrated in Arizona, where in 1996 voters approved a drug-liberalization ballot initiative. The initiative would have required the release of all inmates sentenced for first-time drug offenses—about 1,000 inmates in all. But in 1997, the state legislature amended the law to disqualify from this amnesty all first-time drug inmates previously convicted of a felony. As a result, the number of inmates entitled to freedom shrank to 53. Americans clearly are locking up the right people.

Common sense and empirical knowledge conspire against the thesis that crime rates and incarceration rates are unrelated. After all, the simplest explanation for today's declining crime rates is the simultaneous rise in incarceration rates. In other words, all other things being equal, the removal of known criminals from society *ipso facto* will reduce the crime rate.

How do we test this? First, we look for data on crime rates and incarceration rates. In 1980, America began an unprecedented boom in prison construction. This new space has not gone empty: From 1980 to 1996, the incarceration rate lurched upward 209 percent. Over the same 16 years, there has been a relatively steady decrease in the serious-crime rate—a decrease of 31 percent.

In the 1990s, as word spread on the street that serious crimes would provoke serious punishment, crime rates fell dramatically. From 1991 to 1996, incarceration rates rose 38 percent. The serious-crime rate during the same period fell 22 percent. As more *violent* offenders—murderers, rapists, and the like—were taken out of circulation, the violent-crime rate similarly declined 16 percent.

Prison Reduces Crime

Next we should consider the effect of incarceration on specific crimes. Prison can reduce the crime rate in two ways: (a) by teaching criminals that they will suffer punishment for breaking the law (which deters people from committing crimes), and (b) by removing criminals from society (which incapacitates them). As a result, we would expect to see the strongest relationship between crime rates and incarceration rates for those offenses for which both deterrence and incapacitation are operative.

Except for robberies, violent crimes are not well suited to this type of analysis. Most murders, rapes, and other violent crimes are not committed in a serial fashion. Also, most violent criminals have relatively low recidivism rates. Tough incarceration rates may deter these criminals, but because violent criminals, by and large, do not commit many crimes of the same type, locking them up offers little marginal return in the way of incapacitation.

The most appropriate crime for testing both the deterrence effects and the incapacitation effects of incarceration is burglary. Burglars have the highest recidivism rate of all serious offenders. Nationwide, the recidivism rate for burglary is just under 50 percent. This is higher than even the recidivism rate for drug offenders. If not for incarceration, a very high percentage of burglars would simply keep on burglarizing.

"The removal of known criminals from society . . . will reduce the crime rate."

The data suggest a strong connection between burglary rates and incarceration rates. When the prison-building boom began in 1980, the burglary rate started to descend. Except for the mid-1980s, when the number of drug-related crimes rose, the decline in burglary rates has been steady. The burglary rate dropped 44 percent from 1980 to 1996. In the 1990s, the burglary rate fell 25 percent in just six years. This was, again, during the same period in which the overall incarceration rate rose 38 percent. Deterrence and incapacitation combined to produce an impressive decline in burglary rates.

> *"Those of us who . . . thought that crime rates would continue to rise because of social dissolution should admit that we underestimated the effectiveness of simple punishment."*

The same analysis holds true for robbery rates. Like burglary, robbery—the taking of property from another by force or threat thereof—is a crime typically committed in serial fashion. Robbers, like burglars, have high recidivism rates—the highest recidivism rates of any violent offenders. From 1991 to 1996, robbery rates fell 26 percent (almost identical to the 25 percent decline in the burglary rate). Burglaries and robberies have declined at a faster rate in the 1990s than any other serious crimes.

The Effectiveness of Punishment

We have seen in this decade that when career criminals are sent to prison, crime rates drop. Of course, improved police work, greater community involvement, teenage curfews, and other reforms have reinforced these trends. And the success enjoyed during the 1990s scarcely guarantees future success. Even if the violent-crime rate continued to decline at its current rate, it would take 25 years for America to return to the violent-crime rate it enjoyed in 1960. This is highly unlikely for many reasons, including the cyclical nature of crime rates, the demographic bulge of young men coming of age over the next decade, and the fact that incarceration rates today are still quite low, relative to where they were in the late 1950s.

Still, those of us who, until recently, thought that crime rates would continue to rise because of social dissolution should admit that we underestimated the effectiveness of simple punishment. Americans may cherish many of the wrong values today, but at least we love our lives and property enough to be willing to lock up large numbers of criminals in expensive, out-of-the-way places. Criminals, as a result, are learning that society means business. As long as we drive this lesson home—and as long as America as a whole is spared the pathologies most acutely associated with the inner city—permanent reductions in our crime rates will be a realistic goal.

Imprisonment Is an Effective Deterrent to Crime

by Morgan Reynolds

About the author: *Morgan Reynolds is director of the Criminal Justice Center of the National Center for Policy Analysis, a nonprofit public policy think tank. He is also a professor of economics at Texas A&M University.*

Prisons have broken the back of our 35-year crime wave. It's about that simple.

An estimated 1.8 million inmates were in prisons and jails at midyear 1998—double the number behind bars a decade earlier. A Justice Department study finds that the average time spent by violent criminals in state prisons rose to 49 months in 1997 from only 43 months in 1993. Prison growth has begun to moderate, however, with 1998's 4.4 percent increase below the average 6.2 percent increase in the 1990s.

Lo and behold, as prisons filled, crime fell. The FBI's crime index has declined for seven straight years. Every category of crime is lower than in 1991. The national murder rate is down by more than one-third and down an astounding 70 percent in New York City, the lowest since 1964. In 1995, almost 22,000 people were murdered, a majority of them African-American. In 1998, only 17,000 went to their graves as homicides. Robberies reported to the police have declined by more than 100,000 crimes in only three years. In much of the nation, crime is lower than at any time since the 1960s and almost everyone feels safer.

More Prisoners, Less Crime

In 1991 Eugene Methvin, a highly regarded crime analyst, calculated that about 75,000 new, hard-core, violent repeaters were added to our population every year. Locking all of them up from their third-felony conviction until age 30 would boost the prison population to 1.2 million, our total in 1999. Methvin concluded that this would produce "a sharp drop in our horrendous crime rates." While the justice system undoubtedly has been less efficient in its selection of offenders than his calculation demanded, Methvin's prediction nevertheless has been confirmed.

How could locking up almost one million more bad guys for longer terms fail to cut crime? It's difficult to deny this proposition, but count on the experts to try. They would have us believe that if we released nearly a million inmates today, it would have no impact on crime.

> *"Crime has become less attractive, and adults . . . are avoiding entry into the industry or fleeing it."*

Instead of common sense, the elite express caution, celebrate complexity or push obscure explanations for the drop in crime—anything to avoid the conclusion that getting tough works by changing criminal choices. Alfred Blumstein, a criminologist at Carnegie-Mellon University in Pittsburgh, labels the connection between falling crime and filling prisons "too simplistic." Apparently, only complicated stuff is good. Pointing out the obvious is bad form.

Bad Consequences for Bad Choices

As with educational theory, criminology long has been a field driven by fads. Lacking a solid intellectual anchor and populated primarily by sociologists, criminology for the most part has ignored the impact of law enforcement on crime because it was assumed that the risks of punishment didn't enter into offenders' calculations. In fact, most social scientists avoid the word "choice" or calculation in favor of terms such as "precursor," "correlate," "at risk" and influence. Journalists duly follow.

Sometimes, however, a serious academic strays into the real world of criminal behavior. The late psychologist Richard Herrnstein, for example, wrote that the real cause of crime is "people for whom the positive side of the ledger sufficiently outweighs the negative side and who have the opportunity for breaking the law."

The "negative side" of the ledger is exactly what the criminal-justice system is supposed to do: Mete out appropriately bad consequences for bad choices. For a nation dedicated to individual freedom, individual responsibility and equality before the law, denial of liberty for thugs is fitting punishment. The system actually is taking this job seriously again, and it is working. Crime has become less attractive, and adults (at least) are avoiding entry into the industry or fleeing it.

Even the *New York Times* concedes that "a remarkably optimistic new view of crime prevention is emerging among experts, and their revised consensus suggests that law enforcement may make a critical difference after all."

In 1950, the odds of going to prison for a serious crime of violence or burglary were 5.3 percent, and crime was low. By 1970, the odds had collapsed to

1.3 percent and, by the end of the decade, had recovered to only 1.6 percent. In fact, during the crime explosion of the 1960s and 1970s, the absolute number of new-adult commitments to prisons for serious crimes of violence and burglary actually declined, while the number of such crimes reported to the police nearly tripled. The system became a bad joke. By 1990, however, the odds of prison time had increased to 2.4 percent and, by 1997, to 2.9 percent.

Expected punishment has been boosted at each stage of the criminal-justice process. In some neighborhoods, community-oriented policing has restored trust between citizens and police, leading to more arrests. Aggressive enforcement against minor infractions has allowed police to charge suspects with more serious crimes based on outstanding warrants for arrest.

Additional prosecutors backed by tougher laws have raised conviction rates. New-prison construction has allowed officials to make convicts serve more of their sentences.

Many criminologists oppose punishment on ideological rather than logical or evidential grounds, believing it cruel and outmoded. Supposedly, only rehabilitation is good. Yet, except for the issue of locking up juveniles, the public never bought into this mumbo jumbo. Almost uniformly across groups, public opinion endorses punishment. More than three-quarters of the public believe that punishment is the primary justification for sentencing. More than 70 percent believe that incarceration is the only sure way to prevent future crimes, and more than three-quarters believe that the courts are too easy on criminals. Three-quarters favor the death penalty for first-degree murder.

> *"Courts have been handing out tougher punishment, and criminals know it."*

The public realizes that nice doesn't always work. There always have been thieves, murderers and rapists and always will be. As long as man is a free moral agent who can choose between good and evil, we'll have evil actions. No amount of rehabilitation, early intervention, personality profiling and therapy will change that.

Punishment Works

Incentives matter in crime just as in other aspects of life. Interviews with criminals provide the strongest evidence that they reason and act much like other human beings. Courts have been handing out tougher punishment, and criminals know it. As more criminals get convicted under new truth-in-sentencing laws, which require convicts to serve 85 percent of their sentences, their sabbatical leaves from society, at taxpayer expense, will lengthen even more.

Seeing that the law means business, many potential criminals decide to stay out of the law's way. As social scientist Charles Murray summed it up recently: "We figured out what to do with criminals. Innovations in policing helped, but the key insight was an old one: Lock 'em up."

Yes, it would be better if young males would straighten up before they become adult criminals. Focus on "prison prevention" rather than prison, as the liberals say. Yet here lies our biggest failure. Studies conclude that punishment works, especially for juveniles, but juvenile systems too often fail to apply the lesson.

Psychologist Sarnoff Mednick of the University of Southern California, for example, compared the records of thousands of young Philadelphia and Danish criminals. He found that 60 percent of those arrested four and five times in Denmark were punished compared with only 14 percent in Philadelphia. "The big problem with our handling of criminals in America is that they're not punished," says Mednick. Many are surprised to hear that, in view of the nation's relatively high number of adult prisons. Yet, often the first time a young man makes his way to jail or prison it is his first punishment, despite an active criminal career with *dozens* of crimes and several arrests.

Leniency Leads to Increased Criminal Behavior

During the 1980s and 1990s, adult crime declined while juvenile crime increased. For example, serious violent crimes committed by adults reached a 25-year low in 1997, according to the annual National Crime Victimization Survey, while the number committed by juveniles remained well above their 1986 low. More dramatically, the arrest rate for violent crimes rose three times faster for juveniles than for adults between 1978 and 1993.

Why? One clue is that youths typically reduce their criminal involvement at the age of majority, suggesting a response to incentives. Apparently, youthful lawbreakers take the prospect of adult jail or prison time more seriously than juvenile sanctions.

This view has been confirmed in a study by economist Steve Levitt of the University of Chicago. Levitt used state data from 1978 to 1993 and found that most of the rise in juvenile crime has been a response to softer and softer treatment of young criminals. The drop in criminal activity at the age of majority is largest in states where the juvenile system is lenient and the adult system is tough. By contrast, criminal activity goes up at the age of majority in states with harsh juvenile courts and lenient adult courts.

States more likely to put youths into secure custody enjoy lower rates of juvenile offending, and the deterrent effect is stronger than that for adults. What seems to matter both to adults and to youth is the current law-enforcement sanctions facing each group, not contemporary sanctions for the other group.

> *"Most of the rise in juvenile crime has been a response to softer and softer treatment of young criminals."*

So are jails and prisons panaceas? Of course not. The infamous "root causes"—poverty, failed public schools and out-of-wedlock births—matter, too. Thirty years ago, one in three African-American babies was born out of wedlock. In 1999, it's seven out of ten, and white illegitimacy rates have jumped to one in four. Billions of federal dollars have—with the best of intentions—subsidized irresponsibility and ruined millions of lives. But the nationwide decline in family, character formation and personal restraint means that external restraints are all the more important.

Many reforms could alleviate our dependence on incarceration, including more responsible parenting, competitive inner-city schools, private restitution for victims and a retreat in the federal government's disastrous war on drugs. But that's another story. The hard reality is that there must be consequences for criminal behavior, and that means prison space.

Incarceration Reduces Crime

by Steve H. Hanke and Howard Baetjer

About the authors: *Steve H. Hanke is a professor of applied economics at Johns Hopkins University. Howard Baetjer is a postdoctoral fellow at Johns Hopkins University.*

The FBI recently released data showing that serious crimes decreased in 1996, continuing a pattern that began in 1992. This might satisfy the statisticians who detect an improving trend, but it won't calm the fears of most Americans. Indeed, polls show that the average citizen worries a lot about crime.

Sensing the public's angst, politicians of all stripes have proposed solutions. Their crime-fighting proposals have come in two forms. One is served up by *incentivists* and the other by *structuralists*. The incentivists claim that more severe punishments reduce crime rates.

The structuralists object to these solutions. They argue that getting tough on crime doesn't work. For the structuralists, the solution to crime lies in criminal rehabilitation and also in the amelioration of the root cause of crime: the breakdown in moral standards and civility in America.

Who's right? The evidence, which is summarized by James Q. Wilson and Richard Herrnstein in *Crime and Human Nature*, overwhelmingly favors the incentivists. Contrary to assertions made by the structuralists, getting tough on crime works and it works rapidly, according to data presented in the book.

The data also suggest that stucturalists err in claiming that criminal rehabilitation works. In actuality, it has a poor track record. The one strong leg structuralists have to stand on is based on their desire to reset the nation's moral compass. This is important. But even if we wear the rosiest of glasses, we cannot be too sanguine about the possibility of changing America's moral standards, at least in the short run.

To reduce crime now, we must change the incentives faced by potential criminals.

As Gary Becker, the University of Chicago's Nobel-laureate economist, has shown, crimes are not irrational acts. Instead, they are voluntarily committed by people who compare the expected benefits of crime with the expected costs. As Meyer Lansky, the infamous Mafia boss, claimed, "I am a businessman." He calculated the benefits and costs of his actions like everyone else.

To the extent that expected benefits outweigh expected costs, more crime will be committed. This commonsense view is consistent with public opinion, the views of criminals themselves, and a large body of statistical research.

Crime and Expected Punishment

So, one way to reduce crime is to lower its expected payoff, where the payoff is the difference between benefits and costs of criminal activity. Public policy can do nothing about the expected benefits of a crime, but it can do a lot about the expected costs.

Those costs can be measured by determining the *expected punishment* associated with various criminal acts. That expected punishment is calculated by first multiplying four probabilities: that of being arrested for a crime after it is committed, that of being prosecuted if arrested, that of being convicted if prosecuted, and that of receiving punishment if convicted. The product of that arithmetic is the probability of being punished.

> **"Getting tough on crime works."**

To complete the calculation of expected punishment, we must next multiply the probability of being punished times the penalty for an offense, which is measured by the length of prison sentences and/or the size of restitution payments.

Consider burglary, for example. Of the burglaries committed, less than 7 percent result in an arrest. Of those arrested, 90 percent are prosecuted. Of those prosecuted, 53 percent are convicted. Of those convicted, 42 percent are sent to prison. If we multiply those probabilities together, we find that a burglar has only a 1.4 percent probability of doing prison time.

Because the average prison time for burglars is 15 months, the technical *expected punishment* is an average of only *6 days* in prison (1.4 percent times 15 months). Consequently, a burglary pays if the prospective thief values the stolen goods more than 6 days of freedom.

The National Center for Policy Analysis in Dallas keeps tabs on trends in expected prison time (the expected punishment) for serious crimes. . . . Several points are worth highlighting:

- Expected punishments, measured by expected prison time, are shockingly light. It's no wonder, according to the figures, that we have so much crime in America.
- The expected punishments were dramatically reduced in the 1960s and '70s. Those were the decades when prisoners' rights were aggressively pursued.

They were also the decades in which America witnessed an explosion in crime rates and the apparent validation of the incentivists' ideas about crime.

• The figures also appear to explain why crime has stayed unacceptably high in the 1980s and '90s. The expected punishments have increased little from their low points in the '70s. Consequently, the expected punishments for all serious crimes, except murder, remain far short of their 1960 levels, at only three months for forcible rape, one month for robbery, 11 days for aggravated assault, and 6 days for burglary.

With the costs of crime so low, it makes sense, on the basis of a rational benefit/cost analysis, that many people choose to engage in a lot of criminal activity.

Many observers, therefore, say that the solution to America's crime problems is obvious: increase the expected costs of engaging in criminal activity. This can be accomplished by raising the likelihood of punishment and the severity of penalties for criminal offenses.

Incarceration Rates and Crime Rates

This conclusion, of course, is not universally accepted. Indeed, many people embrace the structuralist notion that harsh penalties don't reduce crime rates.

To support their beliefs, they point out that between 1973 and 1994 incarceration rates nearly tripled, while the number of reported violent crimes per capita approximately doubled and the rate of reported property crimes rose by about 30 percent. Consequently, they conclude that incarceration isn't an effective method of fighting crime.

But incentivists find this argument unconvincing. It is based, they say, on what the famous statistician George Yule called a "nonsense correlation."

Harvard University economist Steven Levitt demonstrated in the May 1996 issue of the *Quarterly Journal of Economics* that the increased incarceration rates between 1973 and 1994 suppressed what would have been an even greater explosion in crime, absent increased rates of incarceration. Levitt's careful empirical analysis established a strong relationship between increased incarceration rates and reductions in crime.

"Careful empirical analysis established a strong relationship between increased incarceration rates and reductions in crime."

His work shows that if we had imprisoned no additional criminals since 1973, America's violent crime rate would be approximately 70 percent higher today and property crime would be almost 50 percent more frequent. Levitt's research suggests that crime in America has risen since 1973 and stays high because we put *too few* criminals behind bars.

An increase in the prison population reduces all major categories of violent and nonviolent crime. Using the Harvard economist's data, we can tell just how well prisons work. For each 1,000-inmate increase in the prison population,

Levitt's research indicates, the following annual reductions in crime will follow: murders, 4; rapes, 53; assaults, 1,200; robberies, 1,100; burglaries, 2,600; larcenies, 9,200; and auto thefts, 700. On average, about 15 crimes per year are eliminated for each additional prisoner locked up, Levitt says.

Anecdotes from the States

Evidence from California and Texas, our two most populous states, appears to confirm Levitt's analysis. According to Morgan Reynolds of Texas A&M University, California nearly tripled its imprisonment rate in the 1980s, from 98 to 283 prisoners per 100,000 population. The result was a 26 percent reduction in the rate of violent crime and burglary during the decade, from 3,210 to 2,377 per 100,000 population.

Meanwhile, in Texas, the prisoners per 100,000 population increased only modestly, from 210 to 257. Although this 22 percent increase in the incarceration rate slowed the rate of increase in criminal activity, it was too small to reverse the trend. Indeed, the rate of violent crime and burglary increased by 17 percent during the 1980s in Texas, from 2,403 to 2,810 per 100,000 population.

In the 1990s, the policies of California and Texas flip-flopped, with California becoming more lax and Texas becoming much tougher on crime. Between 1990 and 1994, California increased its imprisonment rate only 23 percent, from 311 to 382 prisoners per 100,000 of population. Its crime rate increased also, about 0.5 percent, from 2,391 to 2,405 per 100,000 population.

> *"On average, about 15 crimes per year are eliminated for each additional prisoner locked up."*

At the same time, Texas decided to get tough on crime, increasing its imprisonment rate by 88 percent, from 290 to 545 per 100,000, the highest in the nation. In consequence, the crime rates in Texas fell by 21 percent, from 2,613 to 2,059 per 100,000 population.

Incarceration seems to work in Europe, too. For example, British Home Secretary Michael Howard reports that a reduction in crime rates of 8.5 percent over the last three years has been associated with a 25 percent increase in Britain's prison population over the last three and a half years.

Research by Britain's Home Office also squares with Levitt's findings for America: Keeping a British burglar in prison for a year eliminates between 3 and 13 offenses.

Do Prisons Pay?

Incarceration, therefore, appears to work. But does it pay? Levitt's figures suggest that prisons are among the best public investments America can make. He first estimates the economic benefit to society of keeping bad guys behind bars—that is, the annual amount of damage the average criminal would do if on the loose: $53,900.

From this benefit, Levitt subtracts the annual cost to taxpayers of incarceration, about $30,000 per prisoner. This yields an average net benefit of $23,900 per year for each criminal behind bars.

The economist's study thus shows incarceration to be a bargain. Indeed, it could easily be made more so. If inmates were required to work while in prison, they could pay for at least part of their keep. By reducing the taxpayer-financed costs of prison, prison-work mandates would make incarceration an even more attractive bargain.

"California nearly tripled its imprisonment rate in the 1980s. . . . The result was a 26 percent reduction in the rate of violent crime and burglary."

Many analysts believe that if Americans want to be serious about immediately reducing crime, the solutions are at hand. They say that:

- The probability of punishments should be increased, a goal that can be accomplished by more and better policing and by higher conviction rates.
- The punishments for convicted criminals should be increased by lengthening and/or mandating tough sentences and by requiring restitution for victims. Incidentally, according to the incentivists, tougher, mandated sentences should be imposed on criminals who use guns. This targeted approach to gun control, crime experts say, would reduce use of guns by thugs, without increasing the costs of owning and using guns for legitimate purposes.
- Scarce prison space should be allocated primarily to the most dangerous criminals: those with victims. Lengthened and/or mandated sentences, therefore, should target those who commit the most serious crimes and repeat offenders. It makes little sense to use up prison space for a penny-ante criminal who has committed a burglary for the first time if that precludes locking up a serial rapist. Also, serious criminals and repeat offenders should not qualify for early-release programs, if such programs are employed.
- Prisoners should be required to work, so that some of the costs of prisons could be transferred from law-abiding taxpayers to criminals.

To many, this might all sound rather hard-hearted. But a growing number of analysts believe that this package of incentive-based prescriptions would provide immediate relief.

So much for reducing crime rates today. But what about tomorrow? To answer this question, we must address what many researchers believe to be the root cause of crime: the lack of moral standards.

There is little doubt that a wider embrace of a more socially benevolent moral code would do wonders to reduce crime over time. In the 1930s, for example, when a comparatively rectitudinous culture prevailed, few people bothered to lock their doors and theft was generally petty and rare, despite a context of unemployment and poverty that is unimaginable in our wealthy welfare state. "Do unto others as you would have them do unto you" was the order of the day. People took responsibility and expected to be held accountable for their actions.

If we are to have a successful civil society in the long run, we will have to rebuild moral standards so that the vast majority of people honor contracts, respect the rights and property of others, and generally keep their word.

A blueprint to guide this rebuilding effort is, of course, elusive. But it wouldn't hurt if the chattering classes—starting with politicians and extending to journalists, academics, and entertainment figures—upgraded their own moral standards and led by example.

Increased Incarceration of Criminals Benefits Society

by Dan Lungren

About the author: *Dan Lungren is the former attorney general for California.*

Crime in California is dropping—fast. So far, the 1990s look to be the most promising decade for reducing crime since the state started keeping complete statistics in 1952. Although California suffered—along with the rest of the nation—while the crime rate nearly quadrupled between 1960 and 1980, California is now recording some of the largest crime reductions of any state.

Preliminary crime statistics for 1995 show that the overall crime rate in California fell 8.5 percent; violent crimes dropped 5.5 percent and property crimes fell 10.1 percent. If the trend holds, California will record a third straight year of falling crime in 1996, including a marked acceleration between 1995 and 1996. The hard evidence points to historic decreases in all categories of crime in the state. California is about to set state records for:

- The largest one-year drop in state history in the rate *and* number of crimes;
- The largest two-year decline in the number of crimes;
- The first two-year drop in all major categories of crime (homicide, rape, robbery, aggravated assault, burglary, and motor vehicle theft);
- The largest one-year drop in the number of violent crimes;
- The largest one-year drop in the rate and number of property crimes;
- The largest one-year drop in the number of burglaries;
- The largest one-year drop in the number of motor-vehicle thefts.

What accounts for these astonishing numbers? I would suggest it is in large part due to California's passage of a "three strikes and you're out" law, which has done more to stop revolving-door justice than any other measure in state or federal law. Enacted in 1994 by both popular initiative and legislative action, the law requires a defendant convicted of a felony to serve an indeterminate life sentence when it is proved that he has committed two or more previous felonies defined as "violent" or "serious." Offenders given a life sentence become eligi-

Reprinted, with permission, from "Three Cheers for Three Strikes: California Enjoys a Record Drop in Crime," by Dan Lungren, *Policy Review*, November/December 1996.

ble for parole only after serving 25 years or three times the term that the current conviction would ordinarily warrant, whichever is greater. A "two strikes" provision, part of the same law, requires that when a defendant is convicted of a felony, and has been previously convicted of one "serious or violent" felony, the term of imprisonment is twice the usual sentence provided for the second felony conviction.

In June 1996, the California Supreme Court held in *People v. Romero* that, notwithstanding the ostensible mandatory language of the "three strikes" law, judges retain the discretion to strike or dismiss prior felony convictions; the court's judgement relied on statutory interpretation and the separation of powers. Thus, the state of the law is that while judges have discretion to strike a prior conviction, our district attorneys will still prove prior felony convictions and state courts will still sentence offenders under "three strikes." I have sponsored legislation to narrowly define and restrict the discretion that judges will have in these cases.

Accountability for Criminal Choices

As written and applied, "three strikes" is a model of strict and even-handed justice. It demands accountability, reflects common sense, presents a clear and certain penalty, and uncompromisingly invests in public safety. I like to reflect on former Chief Justice Warren Burger's comments made before an American Bar Association meeting in 1981: "A far greater factor is the deterrent effect of swift and certain consequences: swift arrest, prompt trial, certain penalty and—at some point—finality of judgment." Can anybody believe otherwise? The quotation reflects the chief justice's fundamental understanding that the rule of law affords the complementary blessings of both freedom and responsibility and provides the governing framework in which individual citizens make their individual decisions. The rule of law protects our free will from arbitrary constraints; at the same time, it provides consistency and impartiality to the life of the state and its citizens. What seems obvious in this formula is that as individuals exercise their individual, personal liberties in living their lives and in interacting with others, they also become personally accountable for the choices they make—choices from which clear consequences arise.

> *"The career criminal . . . is being forced to make what should be an easy decision: Either stop committing felonies . . . or spend 25 years to life in prison."*

Yet, many opponents of "three strikes" disagree with the notion of strict personal accountability. Of course, while most of the self-proclaimed experts in criminal justice state their objections on other grounds—they call "three strikes" draconian, ineffective, too broad, too tough, and too expensive—the real theme that resounds in their criticism is that "three strikes" "re-victimizes" persons who already have been "victimized" by the forces of an unfriendly society and an adversarial government. In short, their view is that the targets of "three strikes" are not accountable for their conduct because "complex" forces extrinsic to the individual are the principal causes of criminal activity: poor education, unemployment, a detrimental social situation, or even the law enforcement system. Further, these critics have employed this philosophy to demand that sentencing for convicted criminals be made in light of "mitigating circumstances" and that incarceration should be for "rehabilitative purposes" to redress what society "did" to the inmate.

> *"An offender who has committed a series of violent or serious crimes is likely to commit additional crimes of the same nature."*

The voters of California have rejected this nonsense. And the record shows "three strikes" is doing precisely what the voters demanded when they overwhelmingly passed the initiative, by 72 percent to 28. The career criminal with multiple serious or violent felony convictions is being forced to make what should be an easy decision: Either stop committing felonies and live the remainder of your life in freedom, or spend 25 years to life in prison the next time you are caught and convicted of a felony. The career criminal will be held *personally accountable* for his decisions. Imagine that! When the voters rejected revolving-door justice, they rejected the arguments of apologists that we can divorce negative personal conduct from individual accountability.

Proportional Punishment

The second criticism against "three strikes" by criminal apologists is that the law does not furnish proportionate punishment. These critics focus on the cases in which a habitual felon is charged with a "minor" property or drug offense that qualifies as a third strike. They allege it is wholly improper to impose an indeterminate life sentence for a "minor" crime and that instead the offender should be given special consideration or more lenient treatment. The philosophical approach advocated here is that criminal conduct should be viewed in isolation of past history and surrounding circumstances. If a habitual felon currently commits a crime that is classified as a felony under California law, and he has convictions for two previous "serious" felonies, is it any surprise that Californians want a tougher punishment for the current felony?

Let's examine what constitutes a "serious or violent felony" for a "three strikes" prior conviction: murder or voluntary manslaughter; mayhem; rape; sodomy by force, violence, duress, menace, threat of great bodily injury, or fear of immediate and unlawful bodily injury on the victim or another person; oral copulation by force, violence, duress, et cetera; lewd or lascivious acts on children; felonies with personal use of firearm; attempted murder; assault with intent to commit rape or robbery; assault with a deadly weapon; arson; kidnapping; selling drugs to minors; and many others. If these are not "serious" enough, I would like to know which ones should be dropped as insufficiently serious. When the third strike is but a "minor" felony, such as grand theft or possession of certain drugs for sale, why should society ignore the habitual criminal activity of this offender when sentencing him?

Common sense dictates the answer to this question. First, society does not view crime in a vacuum. As Princeton professor John DiIulio wrote, "Most Americans rightly think in terms of total criminality—the full social and moral weight of an offender's acts against life, liberty, and property. They reject the criminological equivalent of grade inflation—judging plea-bargained-gorged prisoners by their last conviction rather than their overall criminal grade-point average, adult and juvenile." Second, an offender who has committed a series of violent or serious crimes is likely to commit additional crimes of the same nature; wisdom demands that an offender's criminal record be the starting point for determining punishment. Finally, the rule of law demands a response to a lifestyle of destruction and violence. There is nothing disproportionate about giving a harsh sentence to a felon who has not learned from having committed two serious felonies before.

Deterrence Effect

There has been a marked split of opinion, at least in academia, as to how best to prevent crime. On the one hand, some argue that habitual criminal activity can be "cured" by placing offenders in correctional programs that renounce retributive goals and instead stress the redemptive value of education, vocational instruction, and even group therapy. Another school of thought centers on the positive behavioral effects of a system of clear and certain consequences for destructive and criminal behavior. Unfortunately, many in the "redemptive programs" group reject outright the legitimacy of deterrence. The causes of criminal behavior are far too complex, they say, to permit any generalizations about whether individuals will consider legal prohibitions or sanctions when they act and interact in society—especially when they are hungry, ill-housed, under-educated, or emotionally neglected.

> *"I believe certainty of incarceration, for a long and inevitable period . . . has a dramatic effect on the behavior of individuals."*

The value of deterrence, however, is grossly underestimated by these "experts," who have devised no way to prove or disprove its effects. I believe certainty of incarceration, for a long and inevitable period, nonetheless has a dramatic effect on the behavior of individuals. Consider the statement of a veteran homicide detective in the Sacramento police department as to the law's impact: "You hear [the criminals] talking about it all the time. These guys are really squirming. They know what's going on. . . . I've flipped

100 percent," Gregory Gaines told a *Sacramento Bee* reporter. Gaines had just been released from Folsom State Prison with two serious or violent felony convictions—two "strikes"—and told the reporter that many other inmates have decided to heed the warnings of the "three strikes" law. "It's a brand-new me, mainly because of the law. It's going to keep me working, keep my attitude adjusted."

> *"A criminal in prison cannot commit crimes against the general public."*

Perhaps the most interesting statistics track the migratory patterns of felons on parole in California. In the last year before "three strikes" became law in 1994, 226 more paroled felons chose to move to California than moved out. After "three strikes" took effect, the flow reversed: 1,335 more paroled felons chose to leave California in 1995 than to enter. We've gone from being a net importer of paroled felons to a net exporter! Coincidence? Hardly.

Another school of thought seeks to explain the reduction in crime in California solely as a function of social or demographic trends. They argue that a troubled economy breeds more crime. (This ignores that in 1992, 1993, and 1994, overall crime in California dropped even as the state's economy endured one of the worst economic recessions in its history.) They argue that the crime rate falls naturally when the proportion of males in the crime-prone age groups declines. (While this may be part of the explanation, no study we have found supports the notion that "demographic changes" alone drive the crime rate up or down.) Without admitting it, this side in the debate, like some of those in the "redemptive programs" community, believes that tough incarcerative penalties for criminals and tough law-enforcement strategies do not work. In short, they deny the obvious value of deterring crime as a means of preventing it.

Consider the historical experience of no deterrence. California had about 138,000 inmates in its prisons in 1996. When we began our push for a tougher response to crime in the early 1980s—establishing punishment and social incapacitation as the priorities of our penal system—the total inmate population was only 25,000, even though the crime rate reached an all-time high in 1980–81. Our prisons had revolving doors through which career criminals cycled, *undeterred by the prospect of a short prison stint.* Many California inmates viewed a stay in prison as a chance to receive neglected medical and dental care, and to beef up their muscles in the weight yard in preparation for the next "recess" on the outside. "Three strikes" and other tougher laws have begun to change that.

Under the leadership of governors Deukmejian and Wilson and the state's vocal (and often overlooked) victims of crime, California embarked on an active prison building program in conjunction with tougher crime laws and more conservative judges. So where are we now? Today we have 138,000 felons incarcerated in state prisons. Unless you believe that releasing those additional

113,000 felons from our prisons tomorrow would have no effect on the number of crimes committed and that our laws, policies, and promise of punishments have no effect on the number of criminals on our streets and the amount of crime suffered by our state, it is clear that we are beginning to win the fight.

But what if we had not changed our incarceration policies so dramatically? What level of crime might California be suffering from today if the runaway trend of upward crime rates of the 1960s and 1970s had continued unabated? In 1994, California's overall crime rate was 3,147 crimes per 100,000 people. The rate would have reached 4,403 per 100,000 had the trend of the 1970s continued. Between 1995 and 1996—the "three strikes" years—we can estimate the level of crime victimization that would have occurred had our pre–"three strikes" crime rate remained unchanged. In 1995 and 1996, California would have had 907 additional murders, 2,015 additional rapes, 37,256 additional robberies, 11,602 additional aggravated assaults, 92,727 additional burglaries, and 56,991 additional motor vehicle thefts. A RAND Corporation study estimated that rigorous enforcement of "three strikes" will reduce serious felonies committed by adults in California between 22 and 34 percent below what would have occurred had the previous law remained in effect. The authors emphasized that about a third of the felonies eliminated will be violent crimes such as murder, rape, and assaults causing great bodily injury. The other two-thirds will be less violent, but still serious, felonies, including less-injurious assaults, most robberies, and burglaries.

Cost to Society

The critics of "three strikes" also miss another obvious truth: A criminal in prison cannot commit crimes against the general public. In fact, the cost of crimes committed against our citizens is higher than the cost of incarcerating them. The critics are warning that "three strikes"—and all our tougher laws—will cost too much to implement. Yet, according to a 1992 U.S. Department of Justice report on justice expenditures and employment, only three cents of every tax dollar goes to public safety such as police, courts, prisons, jails, and related activities. Perhaps we should question why our priorities have been so backwards. I submit that, strictly analyzed in a cost-benefit perspective, the tough approach to crime is financially sound.

A 1996 study by the National Institute for Justice assessed the costs to society of murders, rapes, robberies,

> *"The costs to society and victims for . . . crime range from $2,940,000 for each murder to $1,400 for each burglary."*

aggravated assaults, and burglaries. The costs included both tangible and intangible costs to the victims, their families, and society, from lost income and medical expenses to pain and suffering and risk of death. The federal study's calculations did not include direct costs to the criminal-justice system, such as police, jail, prosecution, courts, prisons, and the like. The costs to society and victims for each crime range from $2,940,000 for each murder to $1,400 for each burglary. Using these base figures, had California not experienced the post–"three strikes" drop in crime in 1994 and 1995, it would have cost us:

- $2.66 billion for the additional murders;
- $174.3 million for the additional rapes;
- $707.9 million for the additional robberies;
- $108.5 million for the additional aggravated assaults;
- $129.9 million for the additional burglaries.

Clearly, the costs to society of a return to the lenient approach, even in purely fiscal terms (which is obviously not the primary consideration when paired with the human costs of crime) are astronomical. Other approaches to preventing crime have value that I, for one, do not dispute. The move toward community-oriented policing must continue and thrive. California leads the nation in community-oriented policing, a philosophy that enables police officers to work more intensively with citizens in their neighborhoods, rather than scurrying from one 911 call to the next. It, too, costs money, but the investment is worth the up-front costs.

In fact, some critics of "three strikes" argue that the example of New York City, which has enjoyed a steep drop in crime without the benefit of state laws similar to California's, undercuts the case for "three strikes" policies. New York City, however, invested in a comprehensive community-oriented policing program along with a "zero tolerance" policy that requires officers to strictly enforce every possible violation. Like "three strikes," New York City's program costs money—and it works. (New York City has added 7,000 officers since 1990. The entire Los Angeles Police Department totals 8,737; New York City, 37,800.) Ironically, it is deterrence again at work in New York City—the criminals in the city know the police are there and change their behavior accordingly.

> *"The price of allowing . . . offenders to return to a lifestyle of victimizing citizens is too high."*

Unfortunately, we are told that a proportionally large group of young males, currently in their pre-teen years, will soon move into their "crime-prone" years. We should refuse to accept the notion that a high rate of crime will be committed by these youths. A juvenile crime wave is not inevitable, just as our high crime rates of the past were not inevitable. As a society we have to confront the conditions that exacerbate levels of juvenile crime and violence. Our challenge is to implement juvenile crime laws and policies which will deter as many as possible from a life of crime while still incarcerating those teenagers who commit serious violence on our citizens. There is an important place for prevention and intervention programs for our young.

Although "three strikes" will incarcerate more habitual criminals, the costs are justified. The price of allowing these offenders to return to a lifestyle of victimizing citizens is too high. "Three strikes" incapacitates active criminals, who can no longer commit crimes against the public. "Three strikes" removes from our streets the harmful role models these offenders present to our youth and to gang "wannabes." "Three strikes" re-introduces into our collective consciousness a moral imperative that criminal activity should not be tolerated in any way. Most importantly, "three strikes" reduces crime by providing a solid and unquestionable deterrent to criminal behavior. California's sharp decline in crime since 1995 may be attributable to numerous, complex factors, but it is indisputable that "three strikes" has played a major role in reshaping public safety in California, both for law-abiding citizens and for would-be criminals.

The Prison System Does Not Work

by William H. Rentschler

About the author: *William H. Rentschler is the publisher of the* Rentschler Report, *a national journal of independent opinion.*

Americans no longer build soaring cathedrals that stir people's souls. Instead, they build countless grim prisons that smother hope. It is a depressing trade-off.

A single mean, bleak prison cell, with its thin mattress, basic plumbing, 60-watt bulb, and concrete floor, costs beleaguered taxpayers—from Portland, Oregon, to Pensacola, Florida; Portland, Maine, to Albuquerque, New Mexico; and all points in between—a minimum of $45,000 and as much as $125,000 to build.

These are precious tax dollars that could be applied to hot breakfasts for poor kids, updated schoolrooms and textbooks, decent education, care of the infirm elderly and mentally ill, repair of crumbling roads and bridges, and countless other pressing needs. This is merely the beginning of the enormous cost of imprisoning wrongdoers who often do not fit the media profile of slavering brutes, but instead may be young first offenders whose minor, frequently victimless crimes pose no threat or danger to the public.

To cage a human being once the prison cell is built represents a cost of $12–30,000 per prisoner each year from tight state and Federal budgets. Because of its high labor costs, New York City spends $50,000 yearly to keep an inmate in jail. The average annual tab is almost $69,000 for the increasing numbers of older inmates over 55, whose health care and other special needs balloon the bill.

These numbers apply for every year an inmate serves for whatever crime he or she committed. Moreover, they continue forever as a taxpayer penalty, since every cell that exists anywhere in the U.S. is guaranteed to be occupied in a national criminal justice system where overcrowding is a grim, unchanging fact of life, no matter how many new facilities are added. This huge annual burden covers the ever-rising costs of punishing and segregating criminals. Taxpayers are stuck with the bill for warehousing, feeding, clothing, and guarding these convicted felons while they are incarcerated.

In the final decade of the 20th century, prisons in the U.S. have assumed a status of near sanctity, almost like a hallowed monument or cathedral in another era. One who dares oppose the construction of yet another new prison is adjudged "soft on crime," tolerant of severe wrongdoing, and likely, if facing election for public office, doomed to defeat.

> *"To cage a human being . . . represents a cost of $12–30,000 per prisoner each year from tight state and Federal budgets."*

Today in America, there is virtually no enlightened dialogue or consideration of what works and what doesn't in criminal justice, how much should be paid to satisfy the lust to punish, and whether there are better ways to attack such age-old ills. Howard Peters III, director of Illinois' Department of Corrections, has said, "The public needs to understand that prisons aren't free." Yet, he is in the forefront of the drive for a new "super-max" prison to house the deadliest felons convicted in Illinois, even though the state already has three of the toughest institutions in the nation. The reason Peters seeks more space is that the present prisons are about half filled with inmates who logically could be transferred to medium-security facilities or released early without risk to the community.

The Prison Lobby

When a task force appointed by Illinois Governor Jim Edgar proposed the new $60,000,000 state-of-the-art institution early in 1993, he was beset by fiscal woes and unable to meet the state's bills on time. Accordingly, Edgar took a cautionary approach and put the massive project on hold, stating, "It's not enough to be tough on crime. We have to be smart on crime, too." Weeks later, under severe pounding from the prison lobby—those who profit from building, supplying, and staffing jails—and the one-dimensional, lock-'em-up law enforcers, Edgar waffled, urging the General Assembly to go ahead with this gargantuan new house of incarceration. His turn-about has touched off a mad scramble by communities throughout Illinois, whose townspeople see the huge prison as a major source of jobs and local spending, and thus are angling furiously to be chosen as the site for its construction.

Something similar occurred in Florida, where Governor Lawton Chiles caved in under intense pressure from National Rifle Association and car rental lobbyists, along with the State Legislature, and approved a massive prison-building measure, despite opposition from the state's most influential newspapers, civic groups, and tax-conscious residents. On the day of the vote, several small planes, paid for by lobbyists and trailing banners exhorting the legislators to approve the $165,000,000 bill, circled the state capitol as a far-from-subtle reminder of their clout.

The public generally hasn't the foggiest idea of the tremendous long-term tax burden of the nationwide prison binge they generally support. Meanwhile, no politician or prosecutor or prison-builder is about to tell voters anything resembling the truth—that prisons are "bought" by states with debt, typically long-term bonds. As with mortgages, financing charges greatly inflate upfront construction costs, which are fed gingerly to the public and represent only the tip of the vast iceberg of obligation over many years.

Far beyond the construction cost and debt service is the commitment by government to pay operating and maintenance costs for decades to come. The National Council on Crime and Delinquency (NCCD), the premier private research and advocacy agency in the U.S., provides this sobering statistic: Over a 30-year period, roughly the duration of a life sentence, the cost of building and operating a typical prison bed (or cell), including debt service, is approximately $1,300,000. At a time when tax dollars are scarce, precious, and fought over by legislators, lobbyists, and local officials, this nation squanders countless billions on ineffective, self-defeating state and Federal prisons and criminal justice policies that increase, rather than control, reduce, or suppress crime.

America long was accustomed to being first in most measures of economic and human progress. Recently, however, it has "achieved" the "honor" of having the highest rate of incarceration in the world, outdistancing by a comfortable margin every other nation in prison inmates per 100,000 residents. Even more damning, a study by The Sentencing Project, a private prison research organization, showed that four times as many black males per 100,000 are incarcerated in the U.S. as in South Africa. This nation quite literally has created its own version of apartheid. Over all, the U.S. cages three to five times as many of its people as Great Britain, France, and other industrialized nations, according to Barry Krisberg, president of the NCCD.

In the mid 19th century, author Fyodor Dostoyevsky wrote that "the degree of civilization in a society can be judged by entering its prisons." By that measure, and the extent to which it incarcerates people, America must be classified as backward, even barbaric, based on the condition and number of prisons, criminal sentencing and correctional practices, and public attitudes toward crime and punishment. This is especially so because a surprisingly high percentage of the more than 1,000,000 human beings incarcerated in this country on any given day are non-violent first offenders whose crimes are of a relatively minor, non-threatening nature.

A Costly Failure

Prisons are an enormously costly failure for controlling and reducing crime, expensive beyond belief, debilitating, demeaning, counterproductive, dangerous to prison staff and the non-violent majority who are imprisoned, and efficient breeders of even more serious future offenses against society. They simply don't work except to remove from the streets the relatively small percentage of persistently and irrationally violent, dangerous, and repeat offenders.

Despite the costliest prison-building binge in U.S. history over the past decade, which continues apace, there is no room in the system for more convicted criminals. This fetish with locking people up is a scandal that has deprived America of meeting some of its most urgent needs.

Many blame it on the magnitude of the drug problem. Most prison admissions today indeed are drug-related, but the vast majority have little or nothing to do with controlling the drug plague. A high percentage is jailed for low-level possession of drugs, the most minor felony class. Few have prior records of violence. Many are suburban teenagers. Most big fish in the drug trade manage to evade the reach of the law, despite costly, overblown "drug wars."

U.S. judges, contrary to popular myth and mass media overkill, impose harsher, longer sentences than those anywhere else in the world. Nevertheless, they are forced by determinate sentencing laws to impose still longer mandatory sentences, which often make no sense at all and strip judges of their discretionary powers.

Syndicated columnist Garry Wills observes pointedly that "a blind will to be tough rather than intelligent makes us keep overloading this ineffectual system. Put in another way, social vindictiveness is our costliest pleasure." The ranting and raving of those who would bury every wrongdoer behind prison walls bring America no closer to eliminating the terrible ravages of violent crime.

Shorter Prison Terms Are More Effective

California criminologists James Austin and John Irwin, in a paper prepared for the NCCD, argue that "There is only one viable solution that would have an immediate and dramatic impact on prison crowding: shorter prison terms." This, of course, triggers howls of outrage.

Austin led a research study in Illinois which showed the state saved about $50,000,000 by releasing 21,000 carefully screened inmates 90 days early to relieve severe overcrowding. While the program was in effect, the state's crime rate actually declined. Austin, a recipient of the Peter Legins Award from the American Correctional Association, believes such initiatives, on a much wider scale, dramatically could relieve overcrowding and improve the attack on crime at a fraction of the cost. "Political and media harangues about street crime," maintain Austin and Irwin, "have resulted in irrational fear and an excessive, ineffective, punitive response to crime."

"There is virtually no enlightened dialogue or consideration of what works and what doesn't in criminal justice."

"The clamor for more and stronger prisons and stiffer sentences makes no sense," according to Michael J. Mahoney, executive director of Chicago's John Howard Association, a private prison and criminal justice watchdog agency. "We can't build our way out of the crime plague. It's counter-productive and economically impossible. High walls, barbed wire, and armed guards give people a certain sense of security, but it's largely illusory. Very few dangerous criminals are locked up at any one time."

> *"This nation squanders countless billions on ineffective . . . prisons and criminal justice policies that increase, rather than control, reduce, or suppress crime."*

Such conclusions by credible professionals fly in the face of what most people have been led to believe. Prisons have failed to bring about the end of crime.

What long prison terms can accomplish, and usually do, is to turn a minor street miscreant into a hardened lifetime professional. It is time to seek an end to the misguided, self-defeating, enormously costly reliance on prisons and to reject their continued existence, except as the punishment of last resort, to be reserved for violent, dangerous, and chronic offenders.

The Prison-Industrial Complex

U.S. prisons today are desperately, dangerously overcrowded because of the myopia of too many judges, prosecutors, legislators, community leaders, editors, demagogues, and well-meaning, but frightened, citizens who wrongly see prisons as the panacea for escalating crime.

The gauge of success for any undertaking is the achievement of its prime objectives at acceptable cost over a reasonable span of time. The measure of a prison system's success would be the ultimate reduction of crime and the restoration of much of the prison population to law-abiding citizenry. By that standard, prisons have failed dismally, and crime continues to escalate in those countries where such facilities are the cornerstone of the criminal justice process.

In the U.S., running counter to all logic, prisons comprise a "growth industry" that defies recession, functions without competition, creates a vast bureaucracy, draws its clients from a massive government-operated and supported judicial/prosecutorial/criminal justice apparatus, and is ever stimulated by a shadowy, self-seeking "prison/industrial complex." On a smaller, but fast-expanding, scale, this is akin to the vast, powerful "military/industrial complex" a visionary President Dwight D. Eisenhower warned against. Both these institutions maintain a vise-like grip on the White House, Congress, governors' mansions, and state legislatures.

In the U.S., a disproportionate percentage of inmates are young, black, poor, undereducated, and unemployed when they enter prison. When they finally are released—as 95% one day will be—they are likely to be embittered, unskilled, penniless, fearful of the future, bereft of all hope, and trained only to continue along the path of crime. Their aim is to get out and get even. Society bears the burden.

Incarceration Exacerbates Criminal Behavior

by Sasha Abramsky

About the author: *Sasha Abramsky is a freelance writer who lives in New York City.*

Popular perceptions about crime have blurred the boundaries between fact and politically expedient myth. The myth is that the United States is besieged, on a scale never before encountered, by a pathologically criminal underclass. The fact is that we're not. After spiraling upward during the drug wars, murder rates began falling in the mid-1990s; they are lower in 1999 than they were more than twenty years ago. In some cities the murder rate in the late twentieth century is actually lower than it was in the nineteenth century. Nonviolent property-crime rates are in general lower in the United States today than in Great Britain, and are comparable to those in many European countries.

Nevertheless, horror stories have led to calls for longer prison sentences, for the abolition of parole, and for the increasingly punitive treatment of prisoners. The politics of opinion-poll populism has encouraged elected and corrections officials to build isolation units, put more prisons on "lockdown" status (in which prisoners are kept in their cells about twenty-three hours a day), abolish grants that allowed prisoners to study toward diplomas and degrees, and generally make life inside as miserable as possible. Marc Mauer, the assistant director of the Sentencing Project, an advocacy group based in Washington, D.C., says, "Fifty years ago rehabilitation was a primary goal of the system." Nowadays it's not. "The situation we're in now is completely unprecedented," Mauer says. "The number going through the system dwarfs that in any other period in U.S. history and virtually in any other country as well." In 1986, according to figures published in the *Survey of State Prison Inmates* (1991), 175,662 people were serving sentences of more than ten years; five years later 306,006 were serving such sentences. People haven't become more antisocial; their infractions and bad habits are just being punished more ruthlessly. Crime, however, is

Excerpted from "When They Get Out," by Sasha Abramsky, *The Atlantic Monthly*, June 1999. Reprinted by permission of the author.

a complex issue, and responses to it that might instinctively seem sensible, or simply satisfying, may prove deeply counterproductive. Locking ever more people away will in the long run increase the number of Robert Scullys in our midst. Robert Scully grew up near San Diego, in the affluent town of Ocean Beach. From a very early age he used drugs, and before he was a teenager, he had been on the streets and then in juvenile facilities run by the California Youth Authority. From

> *"Popular perceptions about crime have blurred the boundaries between fact and politically expedient myth."*

heroin use and dealing he moved to robbery; by the time he was twenty-two, in the early 1980s, he was in San Quentin. In prison Scully degenerated, eventually using a contraband hacksaw blade to escape from his cell and attacking another inmate with a homemade knife.

The Making of a Sociopath

At about the same time, California began opening what it called maximum-security facilities—dumping grounds for troublesome inmates. Scully wound up in solitary confinement in a prison named Corcoran. The guards there, as recently reported in the *Los Angeles Times*, are alleged to have taken it upon themselves to organize gladiatorial combat among prisoners in the exercise yard; they would sometimes break up the battles by shooting into crowds of prisoners. Scully was shot twice. He was placed in a "security housing unit" cell, where for close to twenty-three hours a day he was deprived of all human interaction. In 1990, soon after the "supermax" prison at Pelican Bay had opened in the redwood forests northeast of the old Victorian timber town of Crescent City, Scully was moved again, into a tiny bare cell with a perforated sheet-metal door and a hatch through which his food was served. In the super-max even exercise was solitary. He stayed there four years. At the time of his release, in 1994, he had spent the previous nine years in isolation. A month later he was arrested for violating parole by consorting with an armed acquaintance, and went straight back to Pelican Bay.

Scully re-emerged on March 24, 1995, by now a human time bomb. He was picked up by Brenda Moore, the girlfriend of a fellow inmate, and they began driving south, along Highway 101, toward San Diego, where Scully was supposed to check in with his parole officer. They never made it. Five days later they arrived in Sebastopol, a town an hour north of San Francisco. There, late at night, they loitered around a restaurant until the owner, fearing a robbery, called the police. The pair drove off to a nearby parking lot. Soon after, as they sat in their truck, Deputy Sheriff Frank Trejo, a middle-aged grandfather looking forward to his retirement, pulled into the lot.

Trejo asked to see the woman's license, and as she fumbled for it, according to investigators, he suddenly found a sawed-off shotgun pointing at his face. He was made to back up until he was between the two vehicles and get on his knees, and Scully shot him in the forehead. Scully and Moore ran across a field, broke into a house, and took a family hostage. The next afternoon, with police surrounding the area, Scully negotiated his surrender.

Robert Scully evolved into a murderer while housed in Pelican Bay. There he experienced some of the harshest confinement conditions known in the democratic world. Highly disturbed to start with, he was kept in a sensory-deprivation box for years on end. Psychologists and psychiatrists called in by his defense team believe that he simply lost the ability to think through the consequences of his actions. He became a creature of brutal and obsessive impulse. At Scully's trial Stuart Grassian, a psychiatrist who has spent much of his career studying the effects of isolation on prisoners, and who has testified in class-action lawsuits against departments of corrections across the country, argued that sensory deprivation and social isolation had caused Scully to regress until he was a violent animal capable only of acting on instinct, with no ability to plan beyond the moment. His incarceration had created what Grassian termed "a tremendous tunnel vision." Pelican Bay Chief Deputy Warden Joe McGrath estimates that every month thirty-five inmates are, like Scully, released from isolation directly back into the community.

The Growing Population of Ex-Felons

Since 1985 America's prison population, not counting the more than half a million people in jails at any one time, has increased by about six or seven percent yearly. Truth-in-sentencing laws mandate that many prisoners serve 85 percent of their sentences before being eligible for parole; all the same, figures over the past decade indicate that on average more than 40 percent of prison inmates are released in any given year. Assuming that these statistical relationships remain constant, we can make certain predictions. In 1995 a total of 463,284 inmates were released. To use a worst-case scenario, some 660,000 will be released in 2000, some 887,000 in 2005, and about 1.2 million in 2010. Even factoring in lower release rates because of three-strikes laws and truth in sentencing, and even taking into account estimates that 60 percent of prisoners have been in prison before, there will still be somewhere around 3.5 million first-time releases between now and 2010, and America by then will still be releasing from half a million to a million people from its prisons each year (not to mention hundreds of thousands more from short stints in jail). That is an awful lot of potential rage coming out of prison to haunt our future. . . .

William Sabol, a researcher at the Urban Institute, a Washington, D.C., think tank, has been studying imprisonment and release statistics for ninety metropolitan areas. Over the next few years he will focus on releases in Baltimore, a city with a very high incarceration rate, exploring the effects of release on different communities. For Sabol, the biggest concern is not that already devastated inner cities will be further damaged but that certain struggling blue-collar areas and middle-class black districts, of whose young men large numbers have been imprisoned during the war on drugs, will be unable to reabsorb the ex-cons while retaining their civic character. "When these men return," Sabol explains, "they're less likely to get jobs and there's a higher likelihood of disruption of the family. What we're interested in is will it tip the scales against those neighborhoods that are marginal?" Faced with a growing population of ex-felons, people with resources will probably flee these communities, thereby expanding the areas of devastation.

Since fewer than 10 percent of prisoners are sentenced to life, we can expect that more than 90 percent of prisoners will be released. Releasing over several decades millions of people who either never acquired job skills or lost their skills in prison, and who will face employers' suspicion, is almost guaranteed to produce localized but considerable economic problems. Currently, among black men aged twenty-five to thirty-four with less than a high school education, the jobless rate is around 50 percent. If those in prison and jail are included, the figure rises above 60 percent. If incarceration rates ever start to drop, and fewer people are entering prison than are being released, then according to the most basic principles of supply and demand, wage levels in areas already suffering chronically high levels of unemployment will plummet as the competition for scarce jobs increases. . . .

Eddie Ellis, a onetime Black Panther who was recently released after serving out a twenty-five-year sentence for murder, believes that the cities are sitting on volcanoes. Now a full-time organizer in the Harlem-based Community Justice Center, Ellis told me when we met that starting around the year 2005, New York is going to see the release of wave after wave of inmates, at the rate of about 30,000 a year, who were incarcerated after 1990. "That's when they began phasing out the programs [education in prison, vocational training, and the like]. By 1994 to 1995 they no longer existed. These are the people we're talking about coming out in such a horrendous condition. The next wave that comes out, we're looking at a serious influx of people into a few communities that not only will devastate these communities but will have a larger consequence for the whole city." The welfare reforms of 1996 drastically curtailed felons' access to welfare money, and specifically barred addicts from access to Medicaid and many drug-rehabilitation programs. Ellis predicts rising epidemics, as ex-prisoners without work or Medicaid spread TB, HIV, and hepatitis.

> *"Locking ever more people away will in the long run increase the number of [convicted murderer] Robert Scullys in our midst."*

To complete a grim picture, wholesale incarceration decimates voter rolls. In all but four states prisoners convicted of felonies lose the right to vote. In more than thirty states they can reapply only when they're off parole. Those who find work while on parole will—like much of the black population of the pre-civil-rights South—be paying taxes into a political system in which they have no say. In California alone close to a quarter of a million people are disenfranchised by such laws.

The situation is even worse in twelve states—almost half of them southern—where a felony can result in disenfranchisement for life. The history of these dis-enfranchisement laws can be traced straight back to the post-Civil War South; because of the disproportion-ate number of black men in prison today, the laws continue to affect not just individuals but the aspirations

> *"[There] is an awful lot of potential rage coming out of prison to haunt our future."*

and political influence of entire communities. In a study released in October 1998, the Sentencing Project and Human Rights Watch, an advocacy group based in New York, reported that throughout the country two percent of adults, or approximately four million people, are disenfranchised; within the black male community the figure is 13 percent, or 1.4 million men. In seven states—Alabama, Florida, Iowa, Mississippi, New Mexico, Virginia, and Wyoming—fully a quarter of all black men are permanently ineligible to vote. In Florida alone 204,600 black men, and in Texas 156,600 black men, have lost the vote.

The political implications for the next century are troubling. Already the inner cities, where on average more than a quarter of young black men are disenfranchised, have seen their power as voting blocs shrivel. And since today's young are tomorrow's old, the problem can only get worse. In 1997 the Justice Department estimated that 29 percent of black males born in 1991 would spend some time in prison. Only four percent of white males would do so. In some cities in the states in which convicted felons are permanently disenfranchised, as older, pre-prison-boom blacks die out, the proportion of black men of all ages who lack the right to vote will rise to about one third by 2020. In certain parts of some southern cities—Houston, Memphis, Miami, and New Orleans, for example—it may be as many as half. Conceivably, an overwhelmingly black town could have an electoral register dominated by a white minority.

Quite simply, mass incarceration followed by mass release into subcitizenship will undermine the great democratic achievements of the past half century. In effect, even if not in intent, after the brief interregnum of the civil-rights years the South, with the rest of the country in tow, is once again moving toward excluding huge numbers of African-Americans from the political process. Marc Mauer, of the Sentencing Project, says, "It's a wonder there's any black representation at all, given the numbers."

Prisons Breed Rage

I met several ex-prisoners in New York City who were putting their lives back together under the auspices of the Fortune Society, a nonprofit organization that runs one of the country's most successful and intensive post-release programs. Some of the people I met had done terrible things; others had merely taken foolish wrong turns. Regardless, talking with them gave each one a human face. It helped me to understand that most of these ex-cons are damaged people with hopes and fears and dreams that perhaps can be coaxed out of them in a nurturing environment like Fortune's.

The most extraordinary of the people I met was a thirty-nine-year-old named Edmond Taylor, who had served a total of eighteen years in a variety of New York's toughest prisons for crimes ranging from drug dealing to violent assault. Out of prison for the past couple of years, Taylor has dedicated himself to change; he works full time as a counselor, helping other prisoners to adjust to life on the outside, and he is regarded by Fortune's executive director, JoAnne Page, as one of her great success stories. Taylor came to meet me straight from counseling a distraught woman who'd been told at a job interview that the company wouldn't hire her because she had a felony conviction. He said, "If I can save just one person a year, I'm happy."

A highly articulate man, more capable than most of understanding what led him into violence and helped to destroy half his life, Taylor explained that he had spent nearly four years in "the box"—some of that time in Clinton Dannemora prison, near the Canadian border, for being what he described as "a vocal critic" of conditions within the prison. Describing his reaction to being released from isolation back into the general prison population, he said, "First there's fear, then there's anger, and the anger takes over. It's violent anger. Very quick. No thought of the magnitude of the consequence of the violence. An individual bumped me, rushing to get to the gym. And I rushed up behind him and hit him with a pipe. He went into a coma." Taylor went straight back into the box. I asked how long it had taken him to recover from isolation. He looked surprised by the question, and said, "Honestly, I've still not recovered. I've been out of isolation five and a half years. Ms. Page is my boss. If she was to confront me when I had a lot on my mind, anger would come up before rational thought. Anger. Strike back. Now it's not so much physical as verbal. In another situation it would cause me to lose my job."

> *"Prisons breed global rage. People come out loaded with so much anger that they're ready to blow up at a touch."*

Then Taylor told me a shameful secret. Shortly after he got out of prison, he was living with his brother. His brother criticized him for some of the attitudes he'd brought out of prison with him. "I felt fed up, and I attacked him," Taylor said. "I grabbed him, choked him, lifted him off his feet, threw him to the ground. I pummeled him, causing him to get several stitches above the eye. I grabbed a kitchen knife—I don't remember any of this; he told me afterward— and put it to his neck and said, 'I should kill you. I hate you.' The realization that I put my hands on my baby brother—the only person at that time who'd ever been in my corner. . . ."

Edmond Taylor sees a future of violent chaos, with a large, uneducated army of enraged ex-cons flooding the streets of the inner cities. JoAnne Page adds, "There's an issue of critical mass. As you lock up a higher percentage of young men in a community, what happens when these guys come out, in terms of role models, crime, the safety of the community? Prisons breed global rage. People come out loaded with so much anger that they're ready to blow up at a touch." She worries that many of them, lacking jobs upon release and having no access to state support, will resort to stealing just to eat. Many will also end up homeless, with their best chance of finding shelter being to commit crimes and return to jail or prison. The Correctional Association of New York estimates that on any given day 3,800 homeless people are in prison at Rikers Island and in other New York City jails.

Without making contingency plans for it—without even realizing it—we are creating a disaster that instead of dissipating over time will accumulate with the years.

Alternatives to Incarceration Would Benefit Society

by David C. Anderson

About the author: *David C. Anderson is the author of* Crime and the Politics of Hysteria: How the Willie Horton Story Changed American Justice.

What's behind the declines in violent crime? The question prompts lively discussion among people coming at a huge social issue from different angles: Some point to random demographic changes, others cite lock-'em-up prison policies; still others, most recently, point to more astute policing. This debate is not exactly a replay of the old argument over root causes versus tough law enforcement. The deep social pathologies that breed crime are still there, and that argument unfortunately remains on hold. Instead, the recent drop in crime rates poses a central strategic issue of criminal justice: Should it be reactive, emphasizing the capture, adjudication, and punishment of criminals after they commit crimes? Or proactive, working to prevent crimes from ever occurring? In principle, this should not be an either/or matter, but limited resources force choices.

Call it the "back-end/front-end" debate. Back-enders, focusing on events at the conclusion of the criminal justice process, favor punishment for its own sake and for its deterrent effects. They like the death penalty, long prison terms, and limited discretion for judges and parole boards who might be tempted to reduce them. Front-enders look for results from the early stages of justice: policing, gun control, drug treatment, and other kinds of alternative (to prison) programs for young offenders. In general, the back-end approach attracts conservatives who like to sound tough; the front-end approach attracts liberals who focus on broader social dynamics.

Which is the better way to fight crime? While the question ought to be pursued seriously—it is richly complex in practical, economic, and moral issues—it became hopelessly politicized during the decade that began around 1985, when crack and guns produced a surge of urban crime and politicians sought ways to exploit the fear it generated. As it turned out, this politics of crime heavily favored back-enders as it produced fervent support for capital punishment and a nationwide movement toward three-strikes and other mandatory-sentencing laws.

A Movement Inspired by Fear

The movement was grounded in valid public anxiety about the level of crime, which no longer could be dismissed as an urban ghetto problem. Millions of middle-class Americans were waking up to the fact that fear had transformed their daily lives. Rising crime imposed surcharges for locks, alarms, and insurance; limited their use of parks, subways, neighborhood streets, and other public places after dark; forced complicated logistics for the supervision and protection of children.

Inevitably, people with narrow agendas sought to exploit the fear. Front-enders lamented the new "iron triangle" that lobbied relentlessly, and effectively, for harsher criminal sentences. Its three components: right-wing Republicans seeking to contrast themselves with "soft-on-crime" Democrats; builders, suppliers, and labor unions that benefited from expanding prison construction; and the National Rifle Association, which reflexively sought to fend off serious gun control with proposals for mandatory terms and sentence enhancements for crimes committed with firearms.

Front-enders sputtered in frustration as lawmakers brushed aside evidence that the fear-driven back-end agenda held no promise of greater crime control, and that it created something close to official racism as it forced disproportionate numbers of young black men into prison. What the front-enders failed to grasp was that the discussion had moved away from crime control, where it belongs, and into uglier, more primitive territory. Simply put, the frightened public gave up on government's ability to prevent crime and turned to other ways of handling its fear.

One of these ways was ad hoc privatization: small armies of security guards for hire; profitable new industries (the Club and Lojack to protect cars; cellular phones with buttons programmed for 911; more sophisticated alarm systems).

> *"How can incarceration of so small a fraction of serious criminals have much effect on the crime rate?"*

Another fear-driven remedy was the demand for revenge, or, more precisely, for "expressive punishments" that put more emphasis on venting collective rage than controlling crime. Thus did huge majorities support the death penalty and longer prison sentences; in addition, millions applauded the caning of a young American for vandalism in Singapore and called for legislation to make corporal punishment possible here. They cheered as state lawmakers revived chain gangs and convict stripes and sought to eliminate the "amenities" of prison life. Sensing the public mood, lower-court judges toyed with public "shaming" as an alternative to jail for misdemeanants. Legislators, relieved that they could satisfy voters without having to control crime, were glad to go along with this use of criminal justice for mass therapy.

Cost-Effective Crime Prevention

While a back-end strategy could guarantee a quick political payoff, no serious policymaker could ignore the longer-term costs. Between 1984 and 1994, according to the Federal Bureau of Justice Statistics, the number of convicts admitted to the nation's state and federal prisons in a year swelled 120 percent, from 246,260 to 541,434, boosting the total incarcerated 116 percent, from 419,346 to 904,647. The taxpayers' overall bill for criminal justice—police, courts, and corrections—also nearly doubled in the period, from $45.6 billion in 1985 to $93.8 billion seven years later, with corrections' share of the total increasing from 28.6 percent to 33.6 percent, or $31.5 billion.

> *"There is simply no escaping the troubling distortion of spending for corrections at the expense of the rest of the system."*

What, in fact, was all this money buying? On this point, the statistics were hardly reassuring. The issue is one of scale. Perhaps half of serious crimes are reported to police. Of these, only about one-fifth result in an arrest. Less than two-thirds of those result in a conviction, and a tiny percentage wind up serving time in a state or federal penitentiary. Thus, the 20 million serious crimes committed each year produce about 500,000 incarcerations—and a third of them are for nonviolent drug offenses or drunk driving. Even if each convicted felon is responsible for many more than one crime apiece, how can incarceration of so small a fraction of serious criminals have much effect on the crime rate, either directly or as a deterrent? And, if budgets are limited, how is it possible to justify spending 33.6 percent of all the available money to impose serious punishment for a tiny percentage of serious crimes?

People determined to promote the back-end strategy point to studies that document crimes and costs apparently saved by incarceration. William Bennett and his co-authors John DiIulio and John Walters refer in their book *Body Count* to surveys of prison inmates in Wisconsin and New Jersey who claim to have committed numerous crimes in the year before their imprisonment. Both groups of inmates self-reported medians of 12 property or violent crimes, excluding drug crimes. The authors quote other research finding as many as 21 averted crimes for each incarcerated prisoner.

They also quote a study that sought to assess not only direct costs to victims but "monetary value of lost quality of life" caused by crime. "Using various measures," the study put prices on individual murders ($2.4 million each), rapes ($60,000), arson ("almost $50,000"), assault ($22,000), and robbery ($25,000). Multiplying numbers like that by the annual "crimes averted" factors found in the studies of inmates yields amounts that dwarf the average annual cost of keeping an inmate in prison (about $20,000).

An Incomplete Picture

However such calculations might provide ammunition for lobbyists of the iron triangle, they remain less than persuasive. Obviously, incarceration incapacitates criminals who are subject to it, and many criminals do commit many crimes per year. But the back-enders leave their audiences with an incomplete picture, for nearly everyone who goes to prison eventually gets released. And given the lack of rehabilitation resoundingly documented by recidivism studies over the years, most of those coming out can be expected to commit new crimes at similar rates. Thus, while 541,434 criminals were sent to prisons in 1994, 456,942 came out, for a net reduction that year of only 84,492 criminals. This does represent an increase over 1984, when 246,260 went in and 221,768 came out, for a net reduction of 24,492. But it's hard to see how incapacitating 60,000 more criminals, a figure that includes nonviolent drug offenders, can have more than a modest impact on serious crime rates even if one believes that each person incapacitated would have committed 10 or 20 crimes in a year. The net incapacitation figure, furthermore, is small enough to be overwhelmed by an increase in the number of young people recruited into lives of drugs, crime, and guns each year, as happened in the late 1980s. And, of course, as legislatures weary of spending tax dollars for prison expansion, allowing the surge of incarceration to level off, the figures will reverse for a time, with more people coming out than going in, for a net increase of criminals on the street.

As for the claim that the aversion of crimes saves society money, front-end strategies could save as much or more. In any case, estimations of crime control savings don't balance public budgets. And so far, the idea of saving taxpayers so much money in averted costs of crime hasn't led conservative back-enders to support hefty tax increases on them to finance more prison construction.

There simply is no escaping the troubling distortion of spending for corrections at the expense of the rest of the system. Couldn't some of the $31.5 billion that goes to lock up a few hundred thousand serious criminals for a few years each be put to better use preventing some of the 20 million serious crimes?

It's also instructive to think of the issue from the neighborhood's point of view. Suppose that crime may be reduced in equal measure and at equal economic cost either by putting a lot of people in prison or by putting more police on the street and developing other front-end programs to intervene with offenders early. Which strategy leaves the community better off?

> *"The community clearly is better off with more police and front-end [preventive] programs than with more people going to prison."*

Increased police presence risks increased abuse of civil liberties by overzealous officers, a problem that inflicts temporary aggravation on some innocent citizens. But sending people to prison inflicts severe, if not calamitous, emotional and financial stress on their innocent spouses, children, and parents. And their neighborhoods suffer the consequences of having to cope with ex-convicts as they return with their employment prospects permanently stunted and their ability to function in family and community life further impaired by the various brutalities of prison.

> *"A front-end agenda of direct prevention [of crime] doesn't mean giving up on root causes."*

Other things being equal, the community clearly is better off with more police and front-end programs than with more people going to prison. In these terms, a strong case could be made for controlling crime with police even if it costs more than controlling it by sending people to prison. Any evidence that the police approach produces greater crime control at lower cost should blow the prison strategy out of the water.

Ounces of Prevention

In a sense, liberals who embrace a front-end law-enforcement strategy are growing up. A crime control agenda based on prevention arguably might include almost any measure that improves education, creates jobs, supplies day care, improves low-income housing, increases access to health care, and otherwise supports poor families. But by ignoring the citizenry's immediate anxiety about personal security, liberals who emphasized only "root causes" seemed hopelessly naive, and ceded the whole crime issue to conservatives. A front-end agenda of direct prevention doesn't mean giving up on root causes. But it does allow those with a more social conception of crime to embrace an approach that has two immense advantages over the back-end response: It is less vengeful—and more effective.

Consider New York City: The violent summer of 1990 prompted the city's first black mayor, David Dinkins, and his police commissioner, Lee Brown, to push a proposal for new police hiring—and a tax to pay for it—through the city council and state legislature. The effective expansion of the department from 25,465 to more than 32,000 officers would turn out to be a gift of immeasurable value to Police Commissioner William Bratton, brought in from Boston by Mayor Rudolph Giuliani, who defeated Dinkins's try for a second term in 1993.

Bratton had previously served as chief of New York City's transit police, where he had experimented with new strategies. Now he returned with large ambitions that he would realize all too well, attracting so much attention for genuine achievement that the mayor, feeling upstaged, forced him out after two-and-a-half years.

Bratton's approach was to disperse responsibility for crime fighting downward to precinct commanders while instituting weekly meetings to hold them strictly accountable for results. In order to measure them, he forced precincts to produce a wealth of statistical data. Police computers began to map out crime and enforcement patterns with unprecedented precision and timeliness—they might show, for example, that reports of shootings on a certain street corner occurred mostly on Fridays and Saturdays after 9 p.m.

Precinct commanders were called to account in weekly "COMSTAT" meetings: Why are there so many shootings on that street corner? What do we know about that location and the people who frequent it? What are you doing to get it under control?

At the same time, the new commissioner found excellent use for the new cops coming out of the academy as a result of the Dinkins/Brown hiring plan. He ordered a citywide campaign against "quality of life" offenses—drinking in public, urinating on the street, making noise, and other forms of rowdiness.

The "Broken Windows" Approach to Policing

Though the endeavor sounded like a public relations stunt, it was deadly serious, with purposes that ran far deeper than simply promoting better manners in public. Bratton was aware of the 1982 *Atlantic Monthly* article "Broken Windows," much discussed in police circles, by James Q. Wilson and George Kelling; it compares a neighborhood where police ignore low-level offenses with a building where the landlord ignores a broken window. As people realize that they can get away with it, they begin to break more windows until the building is destroyed. Wilson and Kelling used the analogy to argue that determined policing of low-level offenses could inhibit serious criminal activity as well.

In New York, in 1994, "quality of life" became the excuse for an aggressive form of patrolling targeted on youthful lowlifes. It generated complaints of harassment even as it drew praise from older residents of troubled neighborhoods. The routine, based on police lawyers' careful study of Supreme Court "stop and frisk" decisions, called for officers to stop and request identification of anyone they suspected of committing an infraction, accepting only government-issued picture ID.

Those not carrying proper ID or found to be the subject of outstanding warrants were taken into custody, driven to the precinct station, and turned over to detectives who interrogated them for whatever they might tell about drug and gun trafficking and recent crimes in the neighborhood. The process added mightily to the flow of fresh information on which to base new operations.

"The successes of police-based approaches to crime control encourage thinking about other front-end measures."

The effects were immediate and dramatic. The number of homicides in the city had begun a gradual decline in the last years of the Dinkins administration. With the arrival of Bratton, COMSTAT, and aggressive patrolling, the homicide rate began a steep decline that appears to be continuing. Only 985 homicides occurred in the city in 1996, a decline of 57 percent from the peak number of 2,262 in 1990.

Bratton declared that he had proved the broken windows theory. His new measures, he said, had inhibited street criminals, causing them to leave their guns and drugs at home. These claims met with skepticism at first. Weren't crime rates going down all over the country? What was so special about New York? And weren't a lot of things beginning to happen that could be reducing crime independently of the police?

> *"There is broad agreement that much crime might be averted if courts were able to intervene with offenders more meaningfully after the first or second minor offense."*

So far, the New York story survives those questions. The nation's big-city homicide rate turned down after 1991 and has continued to fall through 1996. But New York's decline exceeds the national figure. The homicide rate for cities of more than one million fell from 33 per 100,000 in 1991 to 21 per 100,000 in 1995. In New York, the rate fell from 29 per 100,000 to 16 per 100,000 in the same period.

Other explanations for declining crime include the natural maturing and waning of the crack epidemic, shifts in drug market patterns, and demographic changes that leave fewer crime-prone teenagers on city streets. But these more gradual events don't explain the close congruence of sharp declines in New York City's crime and the introduction of Bratton's new management and strategies.

Meanwhile, the only independent analysis so far, conducted by Andrew Karmen at John Jay College of Criminal Justice, offers some striking findings. Karmen found that homicides committed with guns and those committed out of doors fell more sharply than those committed indoors or with other weapons. He also found that homicides declined with the rise of patrol strength and with increases in misdemeanor arrests for quality-of-life offenses. Such findings bolster police claims that their greater numbers and aggressive patrols are inhibiting gun use and street crime.

The calculation of costs and benefits extends well beyond the criminal justice system and crime victims. A city experiencing dramatic declines in crime from policing, as opposed to slight or negligible ones from increased incarceration, becomes more hospitable to tourists and to businesses. And the good news, palpable on every street corner, calms the middle-class homeowners whose periodic bouts of panic about the city's future weaken their stabilizing commitments to neighborhoods and schools.

Street-Smart Intervention

While the New York experience is especially striking given the size of the city and its police department, it isn't unique. Bostonians have recently seen a drastic decline in crime, particularly in gun violence among juveniles. Observers credit a comprehensive police strategy characterized by unprecedented involvement with communities and cooperation among law enforcement agencies. Houston, Dallas, and San Diego have also seen big declines in crime, apparently the result of increased police presence and more aggressive patrolling.

The successes of police-based approaches to crime control encourage thinking about other front-end measures. At least three spring to mind immediately:

Invest More in Early Alternatives

Offenders sentenced to state penitentiaries for serious crimes typically wind up there only after committing a number of lower-level crimes (only some of which come to the attention of the authorities) for which they receive insignificant sentences to lightly supervised probation or "time served"—days already spent in jail awaiting court action. Especially if they are relatively young, offenders get off with such sentences because judges are reluctant to expose them to the routine terrors of penitentiary life for a first or second offense.

There is broad agreement that much crime might be averted if courts were able to intervene with offenders more meaningfully after the first or second minor offense, rather than waiting for them to commit more serious crimes. Yet the nation's overcrowded, underfunded urban arraignment courts are a classic horror show of criminal justice. The heavy workload, burnout, and cynicism among criminal justice workers usually preclude any careful consideration of the offender and the underlying problems—substance abuse, lack of education, family crises—that lead people into low-level criminality.

During the 1990s, a few jurisdictions found the will and the resources to improve lower courts. Some set up "drug courts" where judges sentence drug-abusing offenders to treatment programs, then monitor their progress, retaining the power to incarcerate them for failure. New York City set up a somewhat different model in midtown Manhattan. This "community court" arraigned low-level offenders of all sorts, sentencing them to community service projects in the neighborhood, and referring them to a well-staffed social service office located on the premises.

Innovative efforts of lower courts are enhanced when probation departments are able to help. Agencies that deal with offenders released under court supervision are likely to be as under-resourced as lower courts. Exceptions are found in Phoenix, Arizona, and in the state of Georgia. Both places offer judges probation—managed "ladders" of sanctions—sentencing options that increase in severity from standard probation supervision through "intensive supervision" (lower caseloads), electronic monitoring, and house arrest, up to work release and boot camp programs based in secure residences. Judges greatly appreciate the chance to move offenders up and down the ladder as they demonstrate more or less willingness to behave.

The possibilities are enhanced further as probation departments get creative with alternative sanctions, finding politically acceptable modes. In South Carolina, for example, judges sentence offenders to pay victims restitution rather than serving time in prison. Offenders who don't have a way to pay are sent to secure residences on the grounds of state prisons, then bused out to work each day in private-sector jobs until they earn enough to pay off their sentence amount. Job developers at the centers come up with the placements, typically hard-to-fill minimum-wage slots where employers frustrated by high turnover welcome the restitution center's steady supply of workers, who are dependably sober, drug free, and motivated by the desire for release.

> *"Research suggests that as drug abusers recover from addiction, they recover from criminality as well."*

The restitution centers suggest the potential for public acceptance of front-end programs. Reliable payments of victim compensation defuse much criticism of the non-prison sanction, while the restitution workers' value to local employers builds support for the idea in the business community.

Expand Drug Treatment

The link between substance abuse and criminal behavior remains obvious and research suggests that as drug abusers recover from addiction, they recover from criminality as well. In large measure, the success of a front-end strategy that calls upon judges and probation agencies to do more with offenders in the early stages of their criminal careers depends upon abundant availability of drug treatment.

The goal should be to develop enough treatment slots so that all addicts who voluntarily seek help may obtain it immediately, and so that judges who wish to make treatment part of a sentence package can order an offender to begin at once. This could be accomplished without any need for big new federal or state bureaucracies simply by amending the Medicaid law so that it will reimburse drug addiction therapy provided through free-standing programs rather than in hospitals.

Skeptics point out that the treatment programs have low rates of success. How can one be sure money spent on them doesn't go down the drain? Yet programs that move even, say, 25 percent of clients into long-term recovery may wind up costing less than sending the same offenders to prison for short terms, then returning them to lives of addiction and crime. Furthermore, treatment managers say that an addict may need several attempts at treatment before it "takes." As courts require offenders to try again and again, the success rate increases.

Get Serious About Gun Control

Researchers confirm the police belief that guns in the hands of kids played a central role in the burst of crime that began in 1985. Even so, lobbying of the

National Rifle Association minimized new gun-control legislation during the 1980s and early 1990s. The Brady Bill and the ban on assault weapons, hailed as big symbolic victories, are relatively modest measures. In 1994 and 1995, however, the NRA overreached politically and, by some accounts, financially as well, and its influence began to recede. That makes real gun control look feasible.

A serious gun policy would, at a minimum, require as much of a person who wishes to own and use a gun as of one who wants to own and use a car. Guns should be numbered and registered, with data on guns and owners stored in a computer database instantly accessible by law enforcement agencies.

In addition, gun owners should be licensed, and the burden should be on applicants to demonstrate that they are mentally healthy, have no criminal or spousal abuse records, and have no problems with drugs or alcohol. They should be required to pass written tests on gun law and gun safety as well as practical tests of gun handling on a firing range. And they should have to carry substantial liability insurance. Beyond that, Washington could require manufacturers to build in safety devices like trigger locks that permit use of the gun only by the registered owner, and magnetic strips or computer chips that make guns easier to detect and trace.

> *"Programs that move . . . 25 percent of clients into long-term recovery may wind up costing less than sending the same offenders to prison for short terms."*

Finally, federal law could require that anyone who wants to purchase more than one gun per month make the case for such a need to the local police. Such a law poses no inconvenience to virtually all legitimate gun purchasers, but it could severely inhibit profiteering by gun runners who make legal purchases from retail stores and resell the weapons illegally on the street.

A New Emphasis on Front-End Strategy

How much would a front-end strategy cost? Obviously the expansion of police departments, lower courts, probation agencies, alternative sanctions, drug treatment, and the bureaucracies necessary to enforce new gun laws would require significant spending. The back-end strategy, however, has already committed the nation to billions in new spending as prisons expand and courts fill them with tens of thousands of new inmates. The issue may not be one of coming up with new money so much as engineering a partial shift of funds already in place.

For now, it's enough that police-led victories over crime in New York and other cities revive the front-end/back-end debate and demonstrate an urgent need for research: How are more police used most efficiently? How can lower courts adapt themselves for early intervention and crime control? What are the optimum staffing levels for probation departments? What kinds of alternative sanctions yield the best results? How do different modes of drug treatment work for different kinds of addicts? What would national gun registration and licensing entail and what would be their likely effects?

Such questions, considered marginal where back-end assumptions dominate talk of criminal justice, now belong at the head of the agenda.

Chapter 2

How Should Prisons Treat Inmates?

The Treatment of Inmates: An Overview

by Dana Tofig

About the author: *Dana Tofig is a contributor to the* Hartford Courant.

Correction Officer Charles Robinson stands at the edge of the gymnasium at Cybulski Correctional Institution. From his vantage point, he can see across the room.

In front of him, a handball smacks off a wall of the gym, creating a rhythmic cadence with the grunts of two inmates. Prisoners are shooting hoops on the other end of the expansive room. The metallic clang of weights echoes through the gym.

Some would look at this scene as an example of a weak prison system, full of fun for convicted felons. After many years as a guard, Robinson sees it differently.

"This breaks up a lot of the monotony of the day," he said. "And it relieves some of the stress."

Wardens and correction officials say that weight rooms, basketball hoops, televisions, radios and other pleasantries accomplish two very important tasks inside a prison: They are a powerful management tool, and they occupy prisoners' time.

However, much of the public is fed up with crime, and pictures of basketball hoops and fully stocked libraries in prisons only make them more disgusted. Politicians, in recent years, have tapped into that frustration and called for the elimination of such amenities. In Connecticut, changes have been made, but they have been tempered by the reality that recreation and education serve an important purpose.

It's rhetoric vs. reality in the get-tough-on-crime '90s.

"The people who are in charge of running prisons have a much more practical view of the importance of amenities than outsiders, especially politicians," said Timothy Flanagan, dean of the college of criminal justice at Sam Houston State University in Texas.

"There clearly is a problem with public perception of prison life."

Keeping Inmates on Track

Willie Kelly Keaton Jr. slides large weights onto a big metal bar. Each makes a hollow ring as the platter-sized weights slap together. Keaton lies on the bench and presses more than 300 pounds over his chest several times. When it gets difficult, he grimaces and pushes the weights up two more times.

He leaps up with pride.

When Keaton first entered prison, he was out of shape and addicted to drugs. In prison, he has found God and the weight room. He said his mind and body are fit for the outside world.

"I can bench-press 405 pounds," said Keaton, who now is in another state prison. "It gives me a lot of confidence to know that I can do that. And all the girls like a man with a healthy body." He laughs and flexes a muscle.

In the prison system, inmates are moved around among prisons and among security levels. So, Cybulski, in Somers County, is the kind of place that many want to go to. It's still prison, but there are plenty of activities that help pass the days, or years, and sometimes help the prisoners straighten themselves out.

A variety of classes and programs available at Cybulski help prepare inmates for the free world—which is where a majority of them are heading within a year or two. There are bumper pool and pingpong tables in the dorms, a basketball court, a weight room, televisions and radios on almost every bunk, a library and other recreational and educational facilities.

Not all of Connecticut's prisons are like Cybulski. At Walker Special Management Unit in Suffield, for instance, recreation for higher-security

> *"Much of the public is fed up with crime, and pictures of basketball hoops and fully stocked libraries in prisons only make them more disgusted."*

inmates is a walk around in a cage. And at Northern Correctional Institution in Somers, the state's most secure prison, recreation consists of shuffling in circles around a concrete, open-air pen, in shackles.

Cybulski's inmates are usually charged with less-serious crimes and are fairly close to being released. The amenities they receive are linked to their attending counseling sessions, getting their high school diplomas and following the rules.

The prison's warden believes that recreation, special classes and other privileges help inmates stay on the right track.

"It keeps inmates busy and keeps them focused positive," said warden Sandra Sawicki. "It's a privilege to be here. They know that."

While the gymnasium hums with the sounds of "rec," on the other side of the institution, groups of men take a variety of classes.

Inmate George Gaston recently went through a major test in his job skills class—a mock interview. A teacher and the school principal peppered the would-be job candidate with pointed questions.

Why should we give you this job over other candidates?

"My focus would be on getting the job done," Gaston replied, choosing his words carefully.

Do you have a criminal background?

"Yes, I do, for possession of drugs," Gaston said. "It was an unfortunate experience. But it gave me the opportunity to graduate from community college."

Why won't you offend again? Gaston, who has since been sent to a halfway house and has a job, paused. "I believe incarceration did serve its job as a deterrent."

"Club Med"

In 1994, gubernatorial candidate John G. Rowland stood before blown-up pictures of basketball hoops and an electronic scoreboard at the yet-to-open York Correctional Institution, a women's prison in Niantic.

He blasted the prison as posh and compared it to a Club Med. It was, he said, a shining example of a state that is too soft on its criminals.

"The reality in Connecticut is that we're coddling our prisoners," he said and vowed to change it.

Such words tapped directly into voters' intolerance for crime and helped Rowland into the state's top job. Bashing prison amenities has become a common, and successful, political tactic. The argument resonates with many voters: Prison should not be a place people want to be.

"It can't be fun, like being outside of prison," said state Senator John A. Kissel. "That doesn't seem to mesh with my view of a tough correctional system."

For years, Kissel has been trying to eliminate weightlifting in prisons. Bulked-up inmates are only more dangerous inside and outside the prisons.

"Essentially what you're doing is you're making criminals stronger," Kissel said.

Kissel has not been able to rid the prisons of weightlifting, but some changes have been made in state prison life. Despite Rowland's tough campaign words, the changes have been subtle and thoughtful.

> *"[Cybulski's] warden believes that recreation, special classes and other privileges help inmates stay on the right track."*

"While [the prisons] haven't been turned into medieval dungeons, they certainly aren't as comfortable as they were in the past," said Nuala Forde, a spokeswoman for Rowland. "Prisons are not supposed to be comfortable."

Under state Correction Commissioner John J. Armstrong, some amenities have been eliminated or limited, and others have been linked more closely to a prisoner's behavior and classification within the system.

"We knew we had to change some ways that things in the Department of Correction were done," said Armstrong, a former guard who was one of Rowland's first major appointments.

Smoking has been snuffed out in all prisons, and inmates' access to phones and visits are tied to the security level of the prison they are in and their behavior. A contentious inmate may get no visits. Others may get "non-contact" visits, held through thick glass and over intercom phones, while lower-security, well-behaved inmates can sit at a table with their visitors.

> *"The argument resonates with many voters: Prison should not be a place people want to be."*

Inmates still can purchase televisions at the commissary, but Armstrong said an inmate who misbehaves will have his or her TV packed up and sent home.

"And we'll charge them for the freight," he said.

The idea is to use such privileges as a management tool to control inmate behavior, while helping the prisoners prepare for the outside world.

"Privileges without accountability are not really privileges at all. They're entitlements," Armstrong said. "A system that has no distinction between good behavior and bad behavior is really a bear to manage."

Tent Cities

On the outskirts of Phoenix, rows and rows of army tents are set up. It looks like a military compound, but the people inside are not soldiers—they're sentenced inmates under the command of Sheriff Joe Arpaio.

Nationally, no one has galvanized the "get-tough-on-prisoners" movement like Arpaio.

As the head law enforcer in Arizona's Maricopa County, Arpaio enjoys a legendary reputation for being tough on criminals. He has erected the tent cities to house inmates sentenced to a year or less. There are no frills or niceties.

"Our men and women went to Saudi Arabi [for Operation Desert Storm] and lived in tents, and they didn't even commit a crime," Arpaio said. "Why would someone complain about putting convicted prisoners in tents?"

Twenty inmates bunk in each structure, and dogs with cameras strapped to their backs patrol the perimeter. The inmates have no basketball or weights, no coffee or cigarettes, no television. They eat lots of bologna. It saves money.

When Arpaio's inmates work in the community, they are chained together, and some wear striped prison uniforms.

"That's the way it should be," he said.

Arpaio has been re-elected sheriff—a powerful position in Arizona—and there has been talk of his running for governor. He also has written a book, *The Toughest Sheriff in America.*

"People are fed up with crime, and they want somebody to do something about it instead of talking about it," he said.

But not everyone feels that tent cities are the answer.

Prisoners who are simply warehoused like that will become more anti-social, some argue, and be more of a problem when they are released. Amenities give inmates something to do instead of causing trouble.

"Things like sports, that's just simple common sense. Most people in prison are of a young age and full of energy," said Jenni Gainsborough of the American Civil Liberties Union. "They are going to find some way of releasing it."

Without amenities to provide that release, she said, "prison becomes very difficult to manage, and it becomes very dangerous for the staff that works in there."

Nearly 400 inmates at the tent cities rioted in November 1996, setting fires and holding 11 guards hostage before getting a forum with Arpaio about the conditions at the prison.

Carrots and Sticks

Inmates who have broken the rules at Cybulski find themselves at the desk of Correction Officer Scott Vanoudenhove, pleading their case and asking not to have their privileges revoked.

"Oh yeah, I've seen crying," Vanoudenhove said. "But usually they just whine and whine and whine."

Vanoudenhove can take away some or all of an inmate's privileges or even recommend that an inmate be sent to another, more restrictive, prison.

It's an example of what many prison officials already know—amenities are a great carrot.

"These programs become the carrots and sticks," said Flanagan, Sam Houston's dean of criminal justice. "You eliminate them, you eliminate the carrots and sticks."

Sam Houston State University surveyed more than 800 prison wardens, superintendents and commissioners in 1996 about the usefulness of amenities in prisons. The administrators overwhelmingly supported the presence of recreation, televisions and educational programs inside the prison walls.

The majority of administrators surveyed endorsed the presence of weightlifting equipment, intramural sports, crafts and hobby programs and other activities in their institutions. Less than 25 percent felt televisions, VCRs, radios and musical instruments should be reduced or eliminated.

> *"The idea is to use…privileges as a management tool to control inmate behavior, while helping the prisoners prepare for the outside world."*

"Amenities provide incentives for inmates to stay out of trouble," Flanagan said. "We do need to consider what it's like to work in these institutions."

At Cybulski, one of the harshest punishments meted out by Vanoudenhove is CTQ, or confinement to quarters. An inmate given CTQ must stay in his bunk area, which is about the size of a walk-in closet. No napping is allowed. There's just lots of time to read and think. William Murcelo, 22, recently used the time to catch up on his Bible reading.

Chapter 2

He had been on a work detail to Northern Correctional Institution—a nearby maximum-security prison—and was caught trying to smuggle employee cigarette butts back into Cybulski.

Murcelo, bored and remorseful, said he knew that if he slipped up again, he could be shipped to a higher-security prison and lose many of his privileges permanently. But he swore that wouldn't happen.

"This time, I'm gonna chill down," he said.

Prisons Should Punish Inmates

by Rowland Nethaway

About the author: *Rowland Nethaway is the senior editor of the* Waco Tribune-Herald, *the newspaper of Waco, Texas.*

The porno videotape of mass murderer Richard Speck taking drugs and living it up in prison makes a piercing argument for the death penalty.

Speck says aloud what many law-abiding Americans fear most about their prison systems.

"If they only knew how much fun I was having in here, they would turn me loose," Speck said. Actually, had they only known how much fun he was having in prison, a lot of people would have wanted to take Speck out and shoot him.

Speck was a criminal drifter who broke into a Chicago nurses' dormitory in 1966. He rounded up eight student nurses. He bound and gagged them and took them one at a time to strangle and slash to death with a hunting knife.

He claimed that his butchery was committed in a drug-induced amnesiac state. A jury didn't buy it. Speck, who had been in prison twice in Texas, was sentenced to die. But Speck escaped execution when the Supreme Court struck down the death penalty in 1972. His sentence was commuted to eight consecutive terms of 50 to 150 years each.

The Time of His Life

The videotape of Speck in Illinois' maximum-security Stateville Correctional Center further punctures the hope that criminals are sentenced to prison as punishment for their crimes. Speck is shown along with another inmate snorting cocaine, engaging in various sex acts and bragging about how he has been having the best time of his life while serving time in prison.

Speck did his share of partying before he was arrested as the "sub-animal" who committed what was then described as "the crime of the century."

But in the videotape, Speck brags that he is having more fun in prison than he

outside. His idea of fun is abhorrent to most people, but that's
he point is that the taxpayers don't send criminals to prison to

The two-hour videotape covers two days during which Speck, one of his lovers and the camera operator use the prison's video equipment to make their porno tape. Speck says that he has had more lovers in prison than he can count. He strips off his prison jumpsuit to show his blue women's underwear. He has sex with his lover. He even admits that he committed the killings, which proves that his trial excuse of drug-induced amnesia was a lie.

> *"Taxpayers don't send criminals to prison to have fun."*

Speck died in prison the day before his 50th birthday. The public was told that he died of a heart attack. This new videotape makes one wonder if he didn't die of a drug overdose while partying behind bars with his fellow party animals.

A Comfortable Way of Life

People shouldn't get mad at Speck over the videotape obtained by Chicago's WBBM-TV. And people shouldn't use Speck's outrageous prison behavior as an argument for the death penalty. The point is that lawmakers and prison officials should make sure that prisons are not turned into Club Meds for felons.

Prison becomes a comfortable home and a way of life for many convicts. Once released, they easily return to crime because they do not fear returning to prison. They can shoot baskets, read books, watch color TV, lift weights, renew friendships and eat three nutritious meals a day.

Prison officials say they need the good-time credits, special privileges and amenities to keep convicts happy and prevent them from rioting. But taxpayers don't want happy prisoners.

Taxpayers don't want prison riots, either. But they do want prisoners to feel punished for their crimes. They want prisoners to regret their crimes each and every day and swear that they will do everything in their power to never return to such a living hell. There's a big difference between cruel and unusual punishment and no punishment.

Prisons Should Rehabilitate Inmates

by Joseph A. Califano Jr.

About the author: Joseph A. Califano Jr. is the founder and president of the National Center on Addiction and Substance Abuse at Columbia University in New York City.

From a three-year study of the individuals behind bars in America, I conclude that the predominant national policy of using imprisonment for punishment only is insane—a profligate waste of public funds that endangers public safety, supports the illegal drug market, defies common sense and offends against Christian compassion.

The raw numbers tell an astounding story. Since 1980 America's prison population has more than tripled, from 500,000 to over 1.7 million. Why? The big culprit is drug and alcohol abuse and addiction.

Drug and alcohol abuse and addiction are implicated in the crimes and incarceration of 80 percent—some 1.4 million—of the 1.7 million men and women in U.S. prisons. Those 1.4 million inmates violated drug or alcohol laws, or were "high" at the time they committed their crimes, or stole property to buy drugs or have a history of drug and alcohol abuse and addiction—or had some combination of these characteristics. Among these prisoners are the parents of 2.4 million children, many of them minors.

To protect public safety, individuals who deal in drugs and commit serious violent and property crimes should be incarcerated. But it is just as much in the interest of public safety to rehabilitate those who can be redeemed as it is to keep incorrigibles behind bars.

Today, one of every 144 American adults is in prison for a crime in which drugs and alcohol were involved. Thanks largely to alcohol and drug abuse, the rate of incarceration for American adults was 868 per 100,000 in 1996, compared with less than 100 per 100,000 for most European countries and 47 per 100,000 for Japan. If the current rate of increase continues, one in every 20

Reprinted, with permission, from "A Punishment-Only Policy," by Joseph A. Califano Jr., *America*, February 21, 1998.

Americans born in 1997 will spend some part of his or her life in prison. This will be the case for one in every 11 men and one in every four black men. While today's 130,000 female inmates constitute only 7.7 percent of the prison population, their numbers are rising at twice the rate of increase for male inmates. Drugs and alcohol have also been part of the lives of 80 percent of these women.

Since 1.1 million inmates are in state prisons, 500,000 in local jails supported by states and 100,000 in Federal prisons, it is not surprising that the expense of building and operating prisons is the 800-pound gorilla in most state budgets. With spending rising at a breakneck pace—increasing 28 percent from 1995 to 1996—incarcerating prisoners is the most rapidly growing expense faced by governors and state legislatures. (State and Federal prisons hold individuals sentenced for felonies, which are offenses that carry a sentence of at least one year. About half of local jail inmates have been sentenced for misdemeanors, which carry a sentence of less than one year; the other half are awaiting trial or are held in custody for state or Federal authorities.)

Imprisonment and Recidivism

Criminal recidivism is very much a function of drug and alcohol abuse. The more often an individual is imprisoned, the likelier that inmate is to be a drug or alcohol addict or abuser. Forty-one percent of first-time offenders in state prison have a history of regular drug use; the proportion jumps to 81 percent for those with five or more prior convictions. Regardless of the crimes they commit, individuals who test positive for drugs at the time of arrest have longer criminal records and have been imprisoned more often than those who do not test positive.

Contrary to conventional wisdom and popular myth, alcohol is more tightly linked with violent crimes than crack, cocaine, heroin or any other illegal drug. In state prisons, 21 percent of the inmates convicted of violent crimes were under the influence of alcohol—and no other substance—when they committed those crimes. In contrast, at the time of their crimes only three percent of violent offenders were under the influence of cocaine or crack alone, and only one percent were under the influence of heroin alone. In local jails, 26 percent of the inmates incarcerated for violent crimes were under the influence of alcohol alone at the time of their offense. In contrast, at the time

> *"It is just as much in the interest of public safety to rehabilitate those who can be redeemed as it is to keep incorrigibles behind bars."*

of their crimes only 4 percent of violent offenders were under the influence of cocaine or crack alone, and none were under the influence of heroin alone.

The most troublesome aspect of all these grim statistics is that the nation is doing so little to change them. From 1993 to 1996, as the number of state and Federal inmates needing substance abuse treatment climbed from 688,000 to 840,000, the number of these inmates in treatment hovered around 150,000—

and much of the treatment they received was inadequate. From 1995 to 1996, the number of inmates in treatment actually decreased as the number in need of treatment rose.

Punishment Only Does Not Work

If (as Federal and state laws and regulations provide) the objective of our criminal justice and prison system is to protect the public safety by keeping incorrigible offenders off the street and rehabilitating as many others as possible, the prevailing policy of prison punishment only—with no treatment or preparation for return to the community—is, as Brooklyn District Attorney Charles J. Hynes puts it, "lunacy." For treatable alcohol and drug abusers, mandatory sentences (particularly those that require convicts to serve their entire time in prison with no parole) endanger rather than protect the public safety. Getting and keeping drug and alcohol abusers and addicts in treatment requires all the carrots and sticks society can muster. The hope of early release can encourage inmates to seek and complete treatment; the threat of return to prison can help keep parolees in treatment and aftercare. For these people, the only mandatory sentence that might make any sense would be one that required them to stay in prison until they have completed six months or a year of sobriety.

"Criminal recidivism is very much a function of drug and alcohol abuse."

In the 1990s, the nation experienced a significant reduction in crime. The exhaustive examination of the character of the prison population in *Behind Bars: Substance Abuse and America's Prison Population*, the recent report of the National Center on Addiction and Substance Abuse at Columbia University (CASA), suggests that much of the drop may be due to the increased numbers of substance abusers who are behind bars, thanks to stepped-up law enforcement and tougher prison sentences.

But there is a big caveat. Though many more abusers and addicts are in prison, they will be coming out after, on average, 18 months to four years. Even those convicted of serious offenses like robbery and aggravated assault will be released, on average, in three to four years. Thus, to sustain lower crime rates, we must get as many as possible of these incarcerated addicts and abusers into recovery programs. Indeed, failure to do so will be our nation's greatest missed opportunity for enhancing public safety as it enters the new millennium.

To date, this failure has hit the nation's minorities with special savagery, because they constitute such a high proportion of the inmate population. Blacks, 11 percent of the adult population, comprise 46 percent of state prisoners, 30 percent of Federal prisoners and 42 percent of all prisoners. Hispanics, nine percent of the adult population, comprise 16 percent of state, 28 percent of Federal and 17 percent of all prisoners. Incarcerated in 1996 were 744,678 blacks, 289,956 Hispanics and 619,138 whites. (Whites are 76 percent of the adult population but less than 40 percent of the prison population.) But the common denominator among these inmates is not race or ethnic background. It is drug abuse and addiction. The proportion of state inmates who have a history of regular drug use is essentially the same regardless of race or ethnic background: 61 percent of blacks, 65 percent of Hispanics and 63 percent of whites.

The Benefits of Rehabilitation

It is time to open a second front in the war on crime, and that front is in American prisons. Many of the individuals incarcerated for drug- or alcohol-related crimes would have committed their offenses even in the absence of substance abuse. But many others—hundreds of thousands among the 1.4 million substance-involved inmates—would be law abiding, working, taxpaying citizens and responsible parents if they lived sober lives.

The good news is that an investment in such rehabilitation holds the potential of enormous returns for taxpayers, the economy and crime reduction. The cost of proven treatment for inmates, accompanied by appropriate education, job training and health care, would average about $6,500 per year. For each inmate who successfully completes such treatment and becomes a taxpaying, law-abiding citizen, the annual economic benefit to society—in terms of arrest, prosecution, incarceration and health care costs avoided, along with salary earned and contribution to the economy—is $68,800, a tenfold return on investment in a year. If a year of such comprehensive treatment turns around only 10 percent of those who receive it, it will pay for itself within the next year. Even with difficult prisoners, success rates are likely to reach 20 percent.

There are 1.2 million inmates who are drug and alcohol abusers and addicts. (The remaining 200,000 of the 1.4 million prisoners involved with substance abuse are dealers who do not use drugs.) If we successfully treat and train only 10 percent of those addicts—120,000—the economic benefit in the first year of work after release would be $8.256 billion. That is $456 million more than the $7.8 billion cost of providing treatment and training (at a cost of $6,500 each) for the entire population of 1.2 million inmates with drug and alcohol problems. Thereafter, the nation would receive an economic benefit of some $8 billion for each year those released inmates remain employed and drug- and crime-free.

The potential for reduction in crime is also significant. Estimates of the number of property crimes and violent crimes committed by each active drug addict range from 89 to 191 per year. On a conservative assumption that 100 crimes would be avoided per year by each of the 10,000 drug-addicted inmates who after release stay off drugs and crime, the nation would experience a reduction of one million crimes annually.

Political Rhetoric

Why, then, do we keep following present practices?—because so many politicians spout tough but unrealistic rhetoric that has led our people to believe

(1) that prisons are full of incorrigible psychopaths like those portrayed by Jimmy Cagney and other celluloid gangsters in 1930's films, (2) that treatment does not work and (3) that addiction is a moral weakness that any individual can correct if he or she really wants to. The truth is that prisons are wall-to-wall full of addicts and abusers, that treatment works better than many long-shot cancer therapies and that, like diabetes or hypertension, addiction is a chronic disease that requires continuing treatment.

The United States needs a revolution in the way it views criminal offenders whose core problem is alcohol and drug abuse and addiction. It must answer the call to identify these offenders, to assess the requisites for treatment and training, to separate them from criminal incorrigibles and give them the hand up that can enable them to become productive citizens and responsible parents. If we answer that call, we will save billions of dollars, reduce crime and reclaim thousands of individuals.

What better group to lead that revolution than American Catholics? Twenty years ago a committee of the National Conference of Catholic Bishops wrote, "Correctional institutions should be institutions of rehabilitation . . . [to] help men and women rebuild their lives so that, with few exceptions, they can return to society as considerate, free and law-abiding citizens." Jesus Christ had the experience of being an inmate, and he identified with those who are in prison, saying, "I was in jail and you visited me. . . . Just as you did it to one of the least of these who are members of my family, you did it to me" (Matthew 25:40). Crucified between two men condemned to the same punishment, he promised salvation to the good thief who repented.

> *"Unless . . . inmates are freed of their substance-abuse problems, they are sure to resume their criminal activity promptly after release."*

Inmates who are slaves to drugs and alcohol have a right to help so that they can exercise their free will, repent and rejoin society. In a nation with the world's largest number of incarcerated drug and alcohol addicts, it is hard to think of a higher calling than leading the effort to provide that help. This is a mission to inspire Christians of every sort—from evangelical conservatives to anything-goes universalists.

Pope John Paul II and the Catholic bishops of the United States have called upon the Catholic community to extend its hands and open its heart both to those who are imprisoned and to those who suffer the ravages of substance abuse. If the Catholic bishops want to practice the rhetoric of ecumenism that they preach, then uniting Christians in a massive campaign to change the nation's cruel punishment-only policy for inmates struggling with substance abuse is a perfect vehicle. It is an especially fitting task in light of the accumulating evidence that religion and spirituality are critical components for most inmates who shake their drug and alcohol problems, as Chuck Colson's burgeoning prison ministry is demonstrating.

Prisons are the end of the road for children and teen-agers who grow up in families and neighborhoods wracked by drug and alcohol abuse and addiction. For a generation, on corner after corner in Harlem, Southeast Washington and South Central Los Angeles, we have tolerated drug bazaars and liquor stores that would be wiped out in minutes on the Upper East Side or in Georgetown or Beverly Hills. One way we can repent for letting these training camps for American prisons fester in urban ghettos across the nation is to provide for those drug and alcohol abusers who have been imprisoned. If altruism does not motivate Christian congregations, then self-interest should. Unless these inmates are freed of their substance-abuse problems, they are sure to resume their criminal activity promptly after release.

Inmates Should
Not Be Coddled

by Elizabeth J. Swasey

About the author: *Elizabeth J. Swasey is a contributor to* American Guardian, *the official journal of the National Rifle Association.*

Richard Speck, a drifter convicted of murdering eight student nurses in the summer of 1966 in Chicago, was serving a "life" sentence in the Illinois Statesville Correctional Center. A few years ago, while making an X-rated home movie in prison, Speck turned to the camera and said: "If they knew how much fun I was having, they would turn me loose."

In some prisons today, violent criminals enjoy tennis, basketball, and even handball courts that are so state-of-the-art, few public schools could afford them. Murderers, rapists, and robbers in prison get the type of martial arts lessons that parents pay dearly for every month. And in some prisons, VCR movie rentals are free, as is premium cable TV.

The fact is, many prison luxuries are beyond the reach of working Americans. And while it seems obvious that the standard of living for violent criminals in prison should not be higher than that of the law-abiding poor, it is. Luxuries in prison, not to mention inmate lawsuits seeking more, have raised the cost of imprisonment so that it's now nearly three times the poverty level. This anathema to justice threatens our Second Amendment rights by aiding and abetting those who use the "prisons are too expensive" excuse to take away our firearms civil rights under the guise of crime-fighting.

Misinterpretation of the Eighth Amendment

The road to this sorry state of affairs is paved with good intentions that the abuse-excuse lobby warps into twisted interpretations of the Eighth Amendment to the U.S. Constitution. But it wasn't always this way.

For most of the first 200 years of American history, the Eighth Amendment's prohibition on cruel and unusual punishment banned torture and other barbarous punishments. Then it banned punishment that was disproportionate to the crime, such as a life sentence for stealing a loaf of bread. Then came 1976 and the U.S. Supreme Court's ruling in *Estelle v. Gamble.* In *Estelle,* the Court extended the cruel and unusual standard so that it applied to "conditions of confinement," a.k.a. the inmates' standard of living. And ever since, inmates and their abuse-excuse allies have challenged standards of living in prison as unconstitutional.

Don't ever believe today's prison inmates are a defenseless lot. Prison inmates filed more than 68,000 lawsuits in federal courts in 1996 alone. The nation's incarcerated criminals deluge federal appeals courts with another 17,000 lawsuits annually. Criminals know how to work the system.

Frivolous Lawsuits

For example, a criminal in prison in Utah thought it was cruel and unusual punishment for him to be given tennis shoes that were made by Converse, rather than by L.A. Gear or Reebok. It didn't matter that the sneakers were given to him free; he sued for violation of his constitutional rights under the Eighth Amendment.

A Missouri criminal in prison sued, claiming the lack of salad bars or brunches on weekends was cruel and unusual punishment.

A Nebraska criminal in prison sued, claiming that being served "soggy" toast was cruel and unusual punishment.

In Arkansas, a criminal in prison thought unconstitutionally cruel and unusual punishment was being provided with paper—rather than cloth—napkins. In New York, it was being given a bedspread rather than a blanket. In Pennsylvania, it was being given underwear that was "too tight." One criminal in an Iowa prison even claimed that his "idle pay" (money prisoners receive for simply being in prison) was "insufficient," and thus cruel and unusual punishment.

Prison's High Standard of Living

Compare this list of gripes, snipes, and complaints by violent criminals to a working American who's living life on the straight and narrow at the poverty line. The honest person is considered to have an acceptable standard of living if he gets by on $8,000 a year, the federal poverty line. But not so for murderers, rapists, and child molesters. Their average annual standard of living is $23,000. And even excluding the extra costs criminals require by virtue of their imprisonment—the cost of prison administration, etc.—a standard of living for criminals that is nearly triple that of the working poor is just plain wrong.

> *"Many prison luxuries are beyond the reach of working Americans."*

America needs a minimum standard for prison conditions that is equivalent (less the necessary costs of prison security) to the poverty threshold that is considered acceptable for honest working Americans. In addition to putting an end to manifest injustice, a standard would protect states from constitutional lawsuits over soggy toast.

The National Rifle Association (NRA) CrimeStrike has drafted the "Crime Doesn't Pay Prisons Act," which would establish a minimum standard for prison conditions that states could not fall below, but could rise above. Thus, a prison administrator who chooses to permit certain "perks" in prison to reward good behavior won't be denied.

But neither would convicted murderers, rapists and robbers continue to be better off than many honest men, women, and children. After all, preferential treatment of prisoners over the poor is unheard of in all the world, except in America. Doesn't that make it "cruel and unusual"?

Prisoners Should Not Have Access to Weight Training Facilities

by John P. Zerillo

About the author: *John P. Zerillo is the director of public safety in Mercer County, New Jersey, where he manages two county correctional facilities.*

We should not be transforming those convicted or accused of breaking the law into stronger, criminal machines. Some number of these strength-trained inmates will be discharged and use illicit force to break the law yet again. Strength training and power development will enable inmates to more effectively threaten, hurt, and kill.

There is considerable controversy about whether inmates should be lifting weights in jails and prisons. Some professionals contend that weightlifting is a worthwhile activity for inmates. Others contend that weightlifting endangers the public safety.

A Threat to Public Safety

Weightlifting equipment has been removed from correctional facilities in Arizona, Wisconsin, Utah, Ohio, and Mississippi. Legislators in other states are considering bills to ban weights in correctional institutions. Those in favor of inmate weightlifting point out that inmates who regularly use weights are not usually the troublemakers. The jail administrators often claim that weightlifting is a positive activity because it reduces inmate idleness; it tires them out for when they return to the housing units; it builds self-esteem; it reduces inmate stress; and it teaches self-discipline and goal setting. These advocates contend that all of these are applicable and transferable to other areas of life that will benefit inmates after their release.

My contention is that a policy that permits weightlifting is inconsistent with the public safety that government is charged with maintaining. By using

Reprinted, with permission, from "Build the Minds, Not the Bodies of Dangerous Criminals," by John P. Zerillo, *American Jails*, November/December 1997.

weights, inmates dramatically increase their strength that may be used to threaten or harm individuals. Inmates also use weight equipment as weapons against other inmates and staff, and to damage property. It is not our goal to transform an inmate into a stronger and more physically powerful person while incarcerated.

Many inmates are charged or sentenced for the threat or use of violence as follows:

- simple assault
- homicide
- domestic violence
- sexual or physical abuse of children
- aggravated assault and battery (including assaults on law enforcement officials)
- aggravated sexual assault
- strong-arm robbery (without a weapon)
- resisting arrest
- extortion (by physical force)

Weights Create a Violent Situation

It should also be noted that many inmates who are incarcerated for nonviolent offenses (e.g., possession of a controlled dangerous substance) have a prior record of illicit use of force as well. Furthermore, these offenders have a high recidivism rate. In New Jersey, for example, the recidivism rate is approximately 62 percent. Correctional policy, therefore, should prohibit institutional activities that enhance the potential for violence against weaker individuals. Inmates should be less dangerous upon their release, not more physically intimidating.

Strength-trained inmates also present problems for law enforcement officials. It can be intimidating for a correction officer to be confronted by strength-trained inmates who refuse lawful orders. Restraining and regulating these inmates is a dangerous undertaking and as a result, officer injuries are not uncommon.

"It is not our goal to transform an inmate into a stronger and more physically powerful person while incarcerated."

At the Mercer County Detention and Correctional Centers, Trenton, New Jersey, the medical department estimates that about 50 percent of the injuries treated are attributed to weightlifting. Clearly there are better activities to attract inmates' attention, such as jogging, walking, aerobics, Ping-Pong, volleyball, calisthenics, and basketball.

Furthermore, additional research should be undertaken to ascertain (1) how many inmates are injured lifting weights; (2) how many officers/inmates have been injured in the institutions (as well as costs in lost days and for medical care); (3) how many of these inmates have committed crimes involving the use of personal force or threats; (4) how many inmates committed violent crimes after discharge (as well as the extent that the individual's strength played a role in the offenses); (5) if law enforcement officers encounter problems at the time of arrest due to increased strength of inmates who commit a crime after release; and (6) how often weightlifting equipment has been used within jails and prisons to cause damage to property or persons.

Unless research indicates that there is no significant danger to public safety or property, weightlifting should be prohibited. Meanwhile, inmates can engage in other activities that will increase the likelihood that the inmates will lead law-abiding lives upon discharge. Build the minds, not the bodies, of dangerous inmates!

Weight Training Is a Valuable Rehabilitative Tool

by Jon Marc Taylor

About the author: *Jon Marc Taylor is a prison journalist who has been incarcerated for the past 19 years.*

The debate over the function and purpose of prisons is as old as the concept of incarceration. From the advent of the competing Auburn and Pennsylvania systems to Brockway's Reformatory structure to the Medical Model evolving into the Just Deserts warehousing operation and the current "retributive justice" perspective, society has never settled on what it wants or expects from the act of imprisonment: deterrence, incapacitation, punishment, or rehabilitation—or a combination thereof.

For the past two decades, the pendulum of the use of increasing correctional punitiveness has swung to the right, reaching a crescendo during the last election cycle. Searching for "hot button" topics and "sizzling soundbites," politicians focused on making prison life harsher and starker than it already is to further deter crime and punish those foolish enough to ignore the warning. In this sea of political rhetoric, the rather mundane issue of prison weight training became a local, regional, and national topic.

In March of 1994, first term Congresswoman Deborah Pryce attached an amendment to the Omnibus Crime Bill to ban weightlifting equipment in federal prisons. Pryce commented that "we are supplying a means for many prisoners to significantly increase their strength and bulk, making future acts of violence more likely." The Pryce amendment, however, was not part of the final crime bill signed by the president in September 1994.

One year later, freshman representative Steve Chabot resurrected the amendment in the Violent Criminal Incarceration Act of 1995, which passed the House in February 1996. Even more insidious is that the ban applies to state

Reprinted, with permission, from "The Great Dumbell Theft," by Jon Marc Taylor, *Prison News Service*, Spring 1996.

prisons as well if those jurisdictions receive part of the $10 billion allocated in the crime bill for new prison construction.

Hypocritical Legislation

"Too many criminals spend their time in prison becoming even more violent criminal machines," Chabot said. "We need more books in prison and less weight-lifting equipment." A truly hypocritical statement, since the previous bill took the books out of prison by eliminating federal funding for prisoner higher education by barring inmates from Pell Grant eligibility.

At the state level, South and North Carolina, Florida, and Ohio politicians are considering legislation to remove such equipment from their prisons. Mississippi among other limiting measures, banned inmate weight lifting equipment in a special August 1994 session of the state's legislature. In 1995, Wisconsin inmates lost access to the iron pile by order of Governor Tommy Thompson. Arizona has removed prison weight lifting equipment as well.

In April 1994, Wisconsin's Milwaukee County board of supervisors voted to eliminate all forms of weight training in the county's 1400-inmate prison. Anthony Zielinski, a county supervisor and amateur bodybuilder rationalized the ban stating that "the government should not be in the business of taking criminals and making them

> *"There is strong support among many correctional systems . . . for inmate access to weight training equipment."*

bigger, stronger, and more dangerous and then releasing them upon society."

Even before parole, when "bulked up" ex-cons supposedly would become a danger to society, the issue of inmate access to weight training equipment has been a consideration for the correctional systems. Washington, D.C., officials believe inmates become more aggressive from weight training. In a similar vein, Washington state administrators observe that weights at times are used in a control/power mode.

In May of 1993, a Kansas correctional officer was killed by an inmate wielding a weight. From this and other assaults involving free weights, the department is considering abolishing the exercise equipment from their institutions. North Carolina and Georgia have also reported assaults involving the use of weights. In overall consideration, James Photis of the Law Enforcement Alliance of America quite simply questions, "Why should we be using our tax money to create bulked-up super criminals?"

On the Other Hand

There is strong support among many correctional systems, administrators and line personnel for inmate access to weight training equipment. Federal Bureau of Prisons Director Dr. Kathy Hawk, who opposed the Pryce bill, stated that research demonstrated that weight training was an efficient, inexpensive method of relieving the tremendous pressure of incarceration. Moreover, the director observed, offenders who train with weights "are actually less likely than non-trainers to engage in violence."

Pennsylvania officials reported similar reduced problems with weight lifters, and that assaults with weights were "far less than assaults with kitchen utensils, contraband from shops or maintenance equipment," although weights were by far the easiest item on the list for prisoners to access. Even after parts from a weight machine were used in a Connecticut disturbance, administrators continue to support

> *"In most corrections systems, recreation equipment, including weights, are paid for by the inmates themselves."*

weight training, noting that removing them would create more violence than it would curtail.

Captain A.A. St. Peter of the California Rehabilitation Center at Norco, observed that they had little trouble with prisoners who buffed iron. He said the men developed self-pride, practiced more discipline in their lives, and many had given up drugs to pursue their sport. Quite simply, "through body building," the captain said, "their lives had changed."

Corrections Today, the American Correctional Association's official publication, reported that inmates themselves recognize the importance of weight training. As one prisoner said, through weight lifting "you can take those once uncontrollable desires that got you in trouble and use them in a structured way. You can release aggression and use energy positively. After a year, you might be a different guy."

Finally, in most corrections systems, recreation equipment, including weights, are paid for by the inmates themselves. With profits from the prisoner's canteen and commissary operations (i.e. the company store), prisoners pay for the very equipment that others want to now take away without any mention of remuneration. This act, according to definition—the act of taking away of another's property without his or her consent and with the intention of depriving him of it—is theft. The question then becomes who shall serve the sentence for this crime?

Beyond Rhetoric

Upon release (supposedly the time of greatest danger to the public) the efforts of weight training seem to have the opposite perceived result of rampaging barbarians mugging the man and pummelling the police. Although anecdotal accounts have been reported, Gene Ellebre, president of Bill Glass Prison Ministry conducts hundreds of prison based programs a year involving well-known weight lifters and bodybuilders, among other celebrities and inspirational speakers, cites research revealing that offenders partaking of such self-improvement recidivate at a rate of 32 percent, while those who do not invest themselves in such efforts return to prison at a rate of 75 to 80 percent.

Chapter 2

In his book, *Not Just Pumping Iron*, clinical psychologist Edward L. Smith explains how weight training can provide the way to individual growth. Smith categorizes four evolving motives for weight training: "I should," "I have to," "I want to," and as a "path."

The "I should" lifter works out because someone else wants him to, and quits as soon as the agitator is removed. The "I have to" lifter, in the penal setting at least, would be conceived as an acting out of self-preservation (i.e. bulking up for protection). The "I want to" lifter can evolve from the "I have to" lifter who discovers he likes the challenge or be motivated by some other goal (e.g. athleticism, stress management, etc.). With the progress from consistent effort, Smith explains that weight lifting becomes a "path" for personal growth, that metamorphoses into a way to "confront one's conflicts and fears, and growth."

Dr. Mirella P. Auchus documented psychological evidence of weight training's benefits. Comparing a group of inpatients in traditional group psychotherapy and a group of (non-counseled) out-patients in a study to ascertain the effectiveness of weight training on mental health, the resulting observation was that the same therapeutic progress occurred in both groups. It seems that "discipline and responsibility, problem solving, learning and interest in self care," Auchus noted, spontaneously developed in the out-patient weight training group, even though those traits were not the purpose of the experiment. The experience of weight training improved not only the physical well-being of the out-patient group, but also the traits required to achieve the fitness improved the coping abilities and overall self-esteem of the lifters.

Supporting the scientific analysis, Ron Martiscelli, the recreation director at Florida's Tomoka correctional facility, comments that "the guys that work out have more discipline and self-esteem than just about anyone else in the prison."

In the debate over the potential danger of prisoners training with weights, perhaps Sergeant Andrew Lammers of the Milwaukee House of Corrections puts the concern of paroled and pumped offenders into perspective best. He wryly observes that ex-cons "don't walk into a store, pop out their biceps and say, 'Give me your money!'"

> *"Guys that work out have more discipline and self-esteem than just about anyone else in the prison."*

The real debate, however, is not over prison iron piles. It does not even concern air conditioning, inmates' TVs or prison-earned baccalaureates—all issues recently legislated out of existence. These are all just reactionary push buttons used to manipulate an angry, confused, and purposefully scared public into futile venting of their frustrations onto those they are provided to feast upon—the incarcerated.

Violent Inmates Should Not Be Placed in Super-Max Prisons

by Andy Mager

About the author: *Andy Mager is a freelance writer and activist for peace and justice in Syracuse, New York.*

Locked in a dull colored cell for at least 23 hours daily, unescapable lights, no human contact, besieged with dozens of petty regulations, subject to "arbitrary and excessive use of force by guards." This is the wretched life facing men imprisoned, sometimes for many years, in the Maximum Control Facility (MCF) in Westville and the Secured Housing Unit (SHU) at the Wabash Valley Correctional Facility in Carlisle, Indiana's two super-maximum security prisons. Conditions in these institutions are again under increased scrutiny following the October 1997 release of a damning report by Human Rights Watch (HRW), an internationally respected human rights organization.

Cold Storage: Super-Maximum Security Confinement in Indiana details "cruel, inhuman and degrading treatment" experienced by men in these prisons. HRW concluded that the Indiana Department of Corrections (IDOC) has violated provisions of "the International Covenant on Political and Civil Rights and the UN Standard Minimum Rules for the Treatment of Prisoners" as well as the ban against "cruel and unusual" punishment in the 8th Amendment to the U.S. Constitution. The report underscores the criticisms which began soon after the opening of the MCF in April 1991.

Within a few months nearly half of the prisoners launched a hunger strike to protest "harsh conditions, frequent beatings, and other abuses." This was the first of many such nonviolent protest actions by prisoners. Given their repressive confinement, fasting is one of the only modes of struggle available. In a move designed to further dramatize the desperation of their plight, Kataza Taifa, frustrated at the lack of response to the first hunger strike, severed his fingertip and sent it to

Reprinted, with permission, from "An American Gulag: Indiana's Super-Max Prisons," by Andy Mager, published at www.skbee.com/andy/penSword/PRIS1.HTML.

the American Civil Liberties Union. In May 1992, the Indiana Civil Liberties Union filed a class action suit on behalf of inmates. The resulting 1994 Consent Decree was an early step in correcting some of the worst abuses at the MCF. . . .

Physical Surroundings

While the specifics vary between [MCF and SHU], inmates are basically locked in their cells for at least 23 hours daily. Their concrete enclosures, called "tombs" by some, are approximately 80 square feet and contain a concrete slab bed, desk or table and a sink and toilet. MCF cells have a tiny window and solid doors, while the SHU has no windows and "honey-combed grate" doors which allow in a trickle of light. Some SHU cell doors have special plastic covers to prevent inmates from throwing anything out of the cell. Dim lights are kept on around the clock.

The prisons are "cold, hard and austere" writes HRW, with "a dull sameness in design and color." Critics of similar prisons have labeled them "sensory deprivation" facilities. Correctional officers are stationed in raised control rooms which look down on the housing areas. Each "pod," as they're called, contains cells, showers, a recreation area, a medical examining room and counseling room(s). This allows the prison to limit inmate movement. Video cameras and electronically-controlled gates reduce interactions between guards and inmates.

> *"Every time a prisoner . . . leaves his assigned cell, he is placed in handcuffs (behind his back), with a lead strap (dog leash) held by a guard."*

The arrangement of the cells prevents prisoners from seeing one another from their cells. At SHU, the grates in the doors make it easier for men to yell to one another, allowing for minimal communication, though the yelling bounces off the concrete surfaces creating a terrible din. They eat alone from trays distributed to their cells through a small slot by the guards.

A Day in the Life

"Every time a prisoner on the SHU leaves his assigned cell, he is placed in handcuffs (behind his back), with a lead strap (dog leash) held by a guard," writes [inmate] Balagoon matter of factly. Before the cell door is opened, the prisoner puts his hands through a slot for handcuffing. For trips outside the pod prisoners are also shackled at the legs. At SHU, a recent reform allows movement of some inmates without handcuffing.

Carp, the pen name of a man who began working in the educational program at Wabash Valley in September 1997, describes his reaction to seeing the conditions first hand, "I went into the B-East Supermax today. I'm sick as hell to my stomach and ready to cry." HRW characterized the life of men in the supermaxes thus, "prisoners experience extraordinary social isolation, unremitting idleness, and few educational or vocational opportunities."

Recreation, again alone, occurs in small areas designed to make escape impossible. This also means that there is little sense of contact with the natural world. "Wells," "oversized cells" and "dog runs" are the way that various prisoners have described the areas which contain some exercise equipment. Recreation is generally permitted for a half hour to an hour daily, though at the SHU recreation is cancelled during inclement weather. In response to continued pressure, the IDOC is now considering group recreation for some inmates.

> *"While the institutional guidelines outline reasonable procedures for access to medical care, prisoners regularly complain that treatment is inadequate."*

Ventilation in both prisons is poor, and, in Balagoon's words, "there is something terribly wrong with the water." Food is prepared elsewhere and reheated at the facility. While the institutional guidelines outline reasonable procedures for access to medical care, prisoners regularly complain that treatment is inadequate and slow in coming.

Contact with the outside world is severely limited for men at the SHU and MCF. Visits take place in a small cubicle with the handcuffed and shackled inmate separated from visitors by plexiglass. They talk via telephone, and can make no physical contact. Daily visits are allowed to MCF prisoners, who also have regular access to telephones. At the SHU visits are allowed only once every 14 days and phone calls twice monthly. All phone calls must be collect, making them very expensive for the recipients. These constraints make it difficult for the men to maintain connections with people on the outside, deepening their isolation.

The Use of Excessive Force

The first Superintendent at MCF, Charles Wright, "encouraged and condoned the unnecessary excessive use of physical force," according to Human Rights Watch. Wright, who left the post in mid-1995, "pursued his vision of total control with a single-minded and lawless intensity: beating prisoners into submission on the slightest pretext or provocation. . . . Our research indicates that the misuse of force was rampant in the early years of both facilities, but especially so at the MCF." While HRW believes that improvements have been made, "prisoners at the SHU continue to voice complaints about excessively brutal cell extractions and other incidents of violence."

"Cell extraction" is the term for the forcible removal of a prisoner from a cell. At both facilities teams of "at least five correctional officers wearing body armor, helmets with visors, neck supports, and heavy leather gloves" carry out the removals. While there may be times when such an extreme measure appears to be the only option, in the past it was the method of first resort, with as many as eight per day occurring at the MCF.

In other situations, men are strapped down on their beds to immobilize them. These "four-point restraints" are designed for situations when inmates are suicidal or an imminent threat. Although guidelines are very specific about when and how this measure is to be utilized, its abuse, though perhaps not as extreme as under Wright's tenure at MCF, continues. Mace, teargas and beatings have also been carried out by guards at both facilities.

One inmate told HRW, "When guards only see you in a cage or at the end of a chain, they just can't relate to you as a person." This statement underscores the tense relations between guards and inmates in these institutions. Racism is a significant part of that tension at the SHU in southern Indiana where the guards are overwhelmingly white and African-Americans make up a significant proportion of the prisoners. At MCF, however, the staff is more racially diverse. Racial animosity between prisoners adds to the tremendous stress of life in these institutions.

How Dangerous Are They?

One of the biggest concerns raised about the super-maxes is the length of time which some men are confined in them. IDOC regulations have kept prisoners at MCF for a minimum of two years, and three years at SHU. HRW found at least three prisoners who had been at MCF since it first opened. These lengths of time, in conditions described by some as "sensory deprivation," may be far too long. The American Correctional Association characterizes isolation for "excessively long periods" as "damaging to human beings and counterproductive as a safety measure." Dr. Stuart Grassian, a psychiatrist at Harvard Medical School who has extensively studied solitary confinement, says it "can cause severe psychiatric harm." Federal Judge Thelton Henderson, whose landmark ruling condemned the infamous Pelican Bay prison in California, concluded that prolonged solitary confinement "may press the outer bounds of what most humans can psychologically tolerate."

After assessing the DOC's criteria for placing men in these prisons, HRW was "unconvinced that the criteria and procedures employed in selecting prisoners for placement in these facilities actually separate out those prisoners in need of such extraordinary control measures." In fact, under the rules, a prisoner convicted of a minor crime could end up in a super-max because of violating a variety of prison rules which endangered or threatened no one!

"When guards only see you in a cage or at the end of a chain, they just can't relate to you as a person."

The due process safeguards in the civilian court system are denied to inmates charged with violating the disciplinary code in prison. When the consequences of these hearings are so severe, it is easy to understand why inmates clamor for greater safeguards.

Mentally Ill Inmates

"Absolutely atrocious by any standard," is the way one psychologist described the care provided to the mentally ill in Indiana's prisons to the *Times* of Munster, Indiana. Up to half the inmates incarcerated at the SHU suffer from mental illness. These men are particularly vulnerable to the crushing effects of solitary confinement. Placing mentally ill or vulnerable people in these conditions is "the mental equivalent of putting an asthmatic in a place with little air to breathe," wrote Judge Henderson. A psychotic inmate at SHU told HRW's psychiatrists that he mutilates himself because "the opportunity to be taken out of his cell for medical attention, even if only temporary, was worth the pain."

Unfortunately, the only mental health services available to them are drugs. The presence of so many mentally ill prisoners not only causes great pain for them, but also makes

> *"Mentally ill inmates, whose behavior is at times irrational, often suffer the worst physical abuse by guards."*

the confinement more difficult for the other inmates. Nearly all the prisoners who speak out from inside the control units highlight the plight of their mentally ill brothers. These mentally ill inmates, whose behavior is at times irrational, often suffer the worst physical abuse by guards.

Why?

While the prisons cite security as the justification for these quarantine-like conditions, some of the men experiencing it see a very different motive. Balagoon, who has been imprisoned at SHU since August 1996, describes it as, "controlling and manipulating body, mind and environment to bring about a desired result of self-destructability or total passivity in all targeted subjects. . . . The SHU is responsible for the destruction of a lot of prisoners' health mentally and physically."

Aliasi Khalfani Salim, another man imprisoned at the SHU, says "retaliatory cell strips, macing, direct threats, physical attacks and intimidation become the tools by which fear is projected onto many prisoners." Many African-American prisoners insist that their efforts to improve prison conditions and expose the racism of the criminal justice system lead to their punishment in the supermaxes. "I am being persecuted because of my social, political, religious and moral views," says Balagoon.

Most of the men confined in these facilities will eventually be released. Their experiences while imprisoned not only provide them with few, if any, tools to help them function effectively in society, but for many have embittered them in frightening ways. The psychological scars they carry greatly increase the possibility that they will carry out future acts of violence. "People will be twice or three times as bad when they are released from these facilities," says State Representative Charlie Brown of Gary, one of the few critics of the super-maxes in the state legislature.

There is no transition for inmates whose sentences expire at the MCF or SHU. They are given no opportunity to interact with other inmates or live in a less restrictive environment. Men who have been incarcerated for long periods of time in ordinary prisons have a difficult adjustment on their hands. Releasing men directly from such isolation is asking them to accomplish a nearly impossible task.

Carp was told that "each year 80 inmates are released right from super-max onto the streets." While HRW knows of no studies of what happens with such men, there is strong anecdotal evidence that the results are deadly. . . .

Strong leadership from the IDOC is necessary to stop the sort of abuse which has characterized the control units from their birth. HRW wrote, "without guidance and control by principled authorities, super-maximum security prisons can become as lawless as the prisoners they confine."

The framers of the Indiana State Constitution called for penal laws "founded on the principles of reformation, and not of vindictive justice." It is time for the state to heed that original mandate and transform the control units into places where men can learn skills and prepare to adjust back into society.

Chapter 3

Should Prisons Be Privatized?

Chapter Preface

In order to cope with the rapidly rising prison population generated by the get-tough stance on crime adopted during the 1990s, federal and state governments have had to commit an ever growing portion of government resources to building and maintaining new prisons. To ease the strain on already tight state and federal budgets, some criminal justice officials have hired private corporations to run prisons.

Proponents of private prisons contend that private corporations run prisons at a lower cost than the government. According to Charles W. Thomas, director of the Private Corrections Project at the University of Florida in Gainesville, "Contracting out corrections speeds up new construction, decreases construction costs by 15–25 percent, [and] generates designs that are substantially more efficient than those chosen by bureaucrats." Proponents of private prisons maintain that innovative prison designs used by the private sector allows private prisons to house more inmates while employing fewer corrections officers, thereby eliminating unnecessary salaries. Though private prisons operate with fewer guards than state or federal prisons, supporters insist that they are just as safe as government-run facilities. David J. Theroux, president of the Independent Institute, maintains that "efficient design and building techniques used by private vendors in the construction of prison facilities have . . . not compromised quality. There is today a store of knowledge on how to build prisons that are safer and require less manpower to operate."

Opponents of private prisons, however, argue that many of the private prison industry's cost-cutting techniques compromise prison safety. Critics of prison privatization often point to the Correction Corporation of America's (CCA) prison in Youngstown, Ohio, as proof that private prisons are not safe. In addition to numerous escapes, Youngstown has been plagued with inmate violence. In its first seventeen months of operation, Youngstown experienced thirteen stabbings and two homicides. Critics of private prisons blamed these violent outbreaks on inexperienced prison guards. Because private prison guards are often paid much less and receive fewer benefits than their state and federal counterparts, private prisons have a high rate of employee turnover. This leads to a chronic shortage of experienced prison guards. "If you have a high turnover rate you have less stability. New employees come in; they really don't know what's going on. That leads to conflict with the inmates," declares Alex Friedmann, an inmate at a CCA prison in Tennessee.

The viewpoints in the following chapter examine the debate surrounding the privatization of the prison system.

Privatization Would Improve the Prison System

by Charles H. Logan

About the author: *Charles H. Logan is a professor and associate head of sociology at the University of Connecticut. He is the author of* Private Prisons: Cons and Pros.

For many years now, I have been studying the arguments for and against private prisons. In the process, I have discovered that while each side of the debate has some valid arguments, there is one key principle that is absolutely crucial to thinking clearly about the issues involved. That principle is this: There must be no double standard. When discussing private prisons, it is not enough to identify potential, or even actual, problems. Nor is it helpful to raise questions or concerns about private prisons and then just walk away, as critics so often do, without applying those same questions and concerns to prisons run by the government. For any problems, questions, or concerns to be arguments against privatization, it must be shown that they apply *more* to private than to governmental prisons.

In all my reading, and in all my discussions and debates with others on privatization, however, I can say with confidence that in no area have I found any potential problem with private prisons that is not at least matched by an identical or closely related problem among prisons that are run by the government. Privatization raises no unique or truly new issues for prisons, but it does offer some new solutions. . . .

Cost

Harvard professor John Donahue, a prominent critic of privatization, argues that the scope for cost savings in corrections is very limited. Imprisonment is such a simple, basic arrangement, he says, that there is almost no room for improvements in efficiency. If this argument were correct, there would be little room for variation in public prisons, either in performance or in cost. Since we

Excerpted from "Objections and Refutations," by Charles H. Logan, in *Privatizing Correctional Services* (Vancouver, BC: Fraser Institute, 1998). Reprinted with permission.

know that there *is* variation (great variation) in both of these, it *must* be true that there is *room* for variation.

There are structural differences between the public and private sectors that affect efficiency and cost.

For example, contracting avoids cumbersome and rigid government procurement procedures; private vendors can purchase more quickly, maintain lower inventories, and negotiate better prices and values.

> *"Contracting avoids civil service and other government . . . restrictions that interfere with efficient personnel management."*

Contracting avoids civil service and other government (and sometimes union) restrictions that interfere with efficient personnel management (hiring, firing, promotion, and salary setting; assignment of duties, work schedules, vacations, and leaves; adequate staffing to avoid excessive overtime; delegation of authority; etc.).

Finally, the need to show a profit is a powerful incentive to reduce waste and increase productivity.

Newspaper stories comparing the cost of private vs. government facilities have made claims of savings ranging from 5 percent to 20, 30, or even 50 percent. Little weight should be given to most of these simple comparisons, because they generally compare apples to oranges, and because they ignore the enormous problem of "hidden costs."

A realistic expectation of savings through contracting is probably in the range of five percent to fifteen percent. Support for that statement comes from a study for the National Institute of Justice, based on data provided by the County Auditor of Hamilton County, Tennessee. Because a county auditor is in a good position to identify and estimate hidden costs, such as interagency or indirect costs, this study was unusually thorough.

When Corrections Corporation of America assumed management of the Hamilton County Penal Farm, a 350-bed minimum-to-medium security county prison located near Chattanooga, the facility was inherited in a state of deterioration and neglect and required extensive renovation by the contractor. In addition, that region of the country has relatively low correctional costs and the county was already spending less on its prison than other jurisdictions in the same region were spending on their facilities. Since the county was already among the lowest of the low spenders, this facility provides a fairly severe test of a private contractor's ability to lower costs still further while simultaneously renovating the physical plant, expanding capacity, and improving the quality of operations, all of which it did accomplish.

Consistently conservative assumptions were used to estimate all the direct and indirect costs the county would have incurred if it had retained, or if it resumed, operation of the facility itself. The assumptions were conservative in the sense that they were designed to err in the direction of underestimating the costs of county operation. These costs were then compared to the costs of contractual operation, which included not only the contractor's fee but all the direct and indirect county costs that continued to exist in addition to that fee, including the cost of contract administration and monitoring.

The study concluded that, over the three years examined, the county was cutting its costs of corrections by *at least* 4 percent to 8 percent per year, and more probably by 5 percent to 15 percent.

While that study deserves special attention because of the rigor of its methodology, a considerable and growing body of evidence indicates that privatization produces savings for corrections, just as it does for a wide variety of other governmental operations. Indeed, most contracts are—and all contracts should be—the result of site-specific comparisons between the costs of governmental and private operations. Some jurisdictions even require by law that privatization must achieve a certain level of savings, such as ten percent in Texas and seven percent in Florida. Tennessee law required one contract to demonstrate "at least the same quality of services as the state at a lower cost" or "services superior in quality to those provided by the state at essentially the same cost." A study by the state's Select Oversight Committee found the contract was in fact providing higher quality service at lower cost.

Quality

If private prisons *are* cheaper, say the critics, that can only come at the cost of quality. Corner cutting will occur—meaning poorer food and less of it, fewer services, and cheaper labor with lower professionalism and less training.

Systematic evaluation studies conducted so far, however, have generally been quite positive. An evaluation of a privately contracted secure training school for delinquents produced mixed findings, including a list of 36 positive results and 22 negative results. A survey of inmates at a privately run prison in Tennessee elicited 320 responses, of which 49% were positive, 21% were ambivalent, and 30% were negative. However, prisoners who were able to compare the private management with previous management by the county were overwhelmingly positive (24/28 comparison responses). A third study compared the performances of private juvenile facilities in Massachusetts and of a private prison in Kentucky with matched governmental counterparts. On a substantial majority of performance indicators, the private facilities had at least a small advantage. "By and large, both staff and inmates gave better ratings to the services and programs at the privately-operated facilities; escape rates were lower; there were fewer disturbances by inmates; and in general, staff and offenders felt more comfortable at the privately-operated facilities."

> *"The need to show a profit is a powerful incentive to reduce waste and increase productivity."*

The most comprehensive and carefully structured study to date compared the performances of a private, a state, and a federal women's prison on 333 empirical indicators covering eight dimensions of the quality of confinement, including security, safety, order, care, activity, justice, living conditions, and management. While all three prisons were regarded as having been high in quality, the private prison outscored its two governmental counterparts on nearly every dimension, in some cases by quite substantial margins.

> *"Private prisons are expected to meet high standards, and their high rate of certification is evidence that they do."*

Private facilities are often required by contract to be certified as meeting the standards of the American Correctional Association. Except for the Bureau of Prisons and a few state systems, such as Florida, this is a rare condition among government facilities. Certification does not guarantee quality, but its requirement is evidence that private prisons are expected to meet high standards, and their high rate of certification is evidence that they do.

Other evidence of quality is indirect, such as the fact that contracts are regularly renewed by satisfied government agencies, and the fact that no state is under court orders to rectify poor conditions caused by *private* operations, while the majority of American states *are* under such orders as the result of *governmental* failures.

Quantity

Many critics, especially members of the American Civil Liberties Union (ACLU), are opposed to private prisons largely because they are opposed to prisons generally. If, through efficiency, more prisons are built (argue the critics) they will be filled because they are there.

For over three decades, prison reform groups have advocated a moratorium on all new prison construction, believing that capacity drives use, and hoping that lack of capacity would curtail use. That strategy has backfired, and increasing numbers of prisoners are paying the price in terms of overcrowding and deteriorating physical conditions.

Critics also fear that private prison companies will become powerful lobbyists for harsher punishment, in an attempt to artificially stimulate demand for their product.

Commercial enterprises survive and prosper in the long run not by artificially stimulating a spurious demand for their products, but by accurately anticipating and responding to shifts in real demand. Right now, there is a big overhang of genuine, unmet demand for imprisonment. However, if there is also a demand for alternatives to prison, or if that should grow, commercial companies will be able and willing to respond rapidly to that demand as well. For example, some detention contractors also provide, and aggressively market, electronic monitoring and other alternatives to jail.

One irony must be noted regarding the critics' fear of lobbying. The largest contributor to Pete Wilson's gubernatorial campaign was the California correctional officers union. It wasn't a corporation, but a public employee union, that most strongly backed Wilson in promoting the largest prison expansion program in the country. A study of New York state government found that the great bulk of campaign contributions and lobbying came from the state teachers union, other public employee unions, regulated industry groups such as medical and banking associations, school boards, and the Conference of Mayors. In short, the biggest lobbyist of government is government itself, along with the "nomenklatura" of the government class.

Flexibility

Critics of contracting argue that it is impossible to write a contract that is as broad and flexible as the mission of a public agency needs to be. Contractors may be reluctant to depart from the provisions of their contracts. Renegotiating and changing contracts is time-consuming and terminating a contract is often very difficult. Thus, it may be hard for the government, under contracting, to order and control marginal changes.

This is one of the weaker objections to contracting. It is one of the most widely acknowledged strengths of private prisons that their greater management flexibility and more rapid speed of response promote both minor innovations and major program changes, including initiation, expansion, contraction, or termination.

> *"If there is also a demand for alternatives to prison . . . commercial companies will be able and willing to respond rapidly to that demand."*

In any case, if a particular contract turns out to be too costly or unsatisfactory, it is always possible to terminate it or fail to renew it. In contrast, how feasible is it to replace or halt the activities of government agencies, staffed by tenured and unionized civil servants, whose services are found to be unsatisfactory? It may not always be easy to terminate a contract, but experience has shown that it is nearly impossible to terminate a government agency, even one supposedly made mortal by a sunset law.

Security

What happens in the case of a riot, or a strike? Many times, I have heard critics of private prisons ask this question, then move on to other issues as if it were unanswerable, or required no answer. The answer, however, is about the same as for a government-run prison.

It may be unclear whether or not contracted prison guards would have the *right* to strike, but the absence of such a right has not prevented public guards from engaging in strikes, sickouts, and other job actions. At one point, in a coordinated action, prison guards in Rhode Island and at six penal institutions in Ohio walked off their jobs. In another case, almost all the guards at New York's 33 correctional facilities went out on a strike that lasted 17 days. The Governor called in the National Guard, who were met with violence and property damage by the striking prison guards.

Unemployment as the result of a strike may be a more credible threat to private than to public guards, because a strike or other disruption would allow the government to terminate a contract.

Prison contracts typically include contingency plans to deal with emergencies or disruptions, such as strikes, riots, or bankruptcy. State police and the National Guard provide the ultimate backup for prison staff, whether private or public. A performance bond can be used to defray the government's cost if it has to take control of a contracted facility.

In terms of escapes, the experience of private jails and prisons has been no worse than that of their government-run counterparts. None of the privates, however, has been as lax in its security as the District of Columbia's government-run Oak Hill Youth Center, a high security detention facility for juveniles in Laurel, Maryland, where a journalist's check of the official log showed that 30 percent of the 197 detainees were missing and listed as escapees, or the Prince George's County (Maryland) Jail—much celebrated for its New Generation design—which 11 times during its first year released the wrong prisoners under mistaken identities.

Liability

Critics warn that governments will not escape liability by contracting the administration of their prisons, as some advocates supposedly claim.

To some extent, this is a strawman argument, since I do not know of any private vendor who claims that contracting can *immunize* the government from legal liability. Prisoners in private facilities have at least as many avenues of civil redress as do their fellows in government-run prisons. Total liability, in other words, is not decreased.

However, it is possible that contracting could reduce government's *actual liability exposure*, as opposed to its *legal liability potential*. That is, the financial damages likely to be suffered by government as a result of its legal liabilities can be reduced. Liability exposure can be reduced in several ways:

1. by running prisons better, and thus avoiding lawsuits;
2. by achieving certification, which greatly enhances the defense against lawsuits;
3. by carrying adequate insurance;
4. by agreements in which the contractor defends the government in court and indemnifies it against legal damages;
5. by developing extensive legal expertise and resources, both for preventing and for fighting lawsuits; and

6. by settling quickly out of court, which is easier for private firms than for public agencies.

Accountability

Critics claim that contracting reduces accountability because private actors are insulated from the public and not subject to the same political controls as are government actors. Also, the critics charge, contracting diffuses responsibility; government and private actors can each blame the other when something goes wrong.

Proponents reply that contracting increases accountability because the government is more willing to monitor and control a contractor than it is to monitor and control itself. Contractors—just like their governmental counterparts—are accountable to the law, to governmental supervisors, and ultimately, to the voting public, through the political system. In addition, they are accountable, through a competitive market, to certain forces not faced by government agencies. They are answerable to insurers, investors, stock-

> *"In terms of escapes, the experience of private jails and prisons has been no worse than that of their government-run counterparts."*

holders, and competitors. As a mechanism of accountability and control, the force of market competition is unmatched.

The most obvious form of accountability in corrections, however, is legal accountability. If the Rule of Law can limit and constrain the power of the state, then surely it can hold a private firm at least equally accountable. Constitutional standards, for example, will apply equally to all prisons, whether run by government employees or by contractors.

Corruption

Critics contend that contracting invites corruption, in the form of favoritism, bid-rigging, conflict of interest, bribes, kickbacks, etc. They point to contemporary examples in other areas of contracting, and to historical examples of corruption in contracting for inmate labor.

The historical abuses came at a time when corruption and abuse was much more prevalent in the criminal justice system generally. For example, some states ran their prisons as profit-making enterprises just as ruthlessly and exploitatively without the aid of private contractors as others did with them. In today's political and legal environment, such extreme and flagrant corruption and abuse are very unlikely.

Political corruption is a corollary of government, not just of government contracting. The ingredient common to all instances of corruption is not private ownership, but public power. Payroll padding, nepotism, cronyism, patronage, bribery, payoffs, featherbedding, dishonest budget inflation, conflicts of interest, misuse of public funds, links to organized crime, and many other kinds of corruption also occur within public employee unions and within governmental units that provide services directly, rather than through contracts.

Dependency

Critics worry that contractors will engage in "lowballing," in which they obtain contracts by making unrealistically low bids. Then, when government becomes dependent, the contractor will be free to jack up prices. Worse yet, the contractor may go bankrupt, leaving the government without any correctional capacity.

Market entry costs for single, especially low-security, facilities are well within reach of small businesses or groups of investors. As a new corporation, CCA was able to site, finance, build, and open a 350 bed prison within 7 months, for $5 million. The U.S. Corrections Corporation, founded by two men with an initial investment of $1.9 million, opened its first facility at a seminary purchased for $695,000. If this is all it takes to enter the market, it is well within the resources of numerous potential competitors.

Public agencies can guard against lowballing by evaluating proposed budgets for their realism, rather than just looking for the lowest bidder. Also, regular rebidding of contracts can make lowballing a strategy too costly to pursue. No private company can raise its fees very high above a reasonable profit margin without inviting exposure and opposition by competitors. Competing contractors have the information, motivation, and organizational resources to control each others' prices to a much greater degree than the information, motivation, and resources of taxpayers to control government costs.

The issue of dependence, as an objection to private prisons, has a self-defeating character. If dependence is a real problem, will the problem be solved if there are *no* private vendors? If a public service can only be supplied by government employees, organized into unions, is that not also a form of dependence? To argue that private suppliers of a public service will not be sufficiently competitive is not a very good argument for public monopoly....

Perhaps their most important function of all is that private prisons pro-

> *"Perhaps their most important function of all is that private prisons provide a comparative yardstick against which to measure performance."*

vide a comparative yardstick against which to measure performance. How do we know if the government is running our prisons in the most humane, effective, and efficient manner possible? As with any service, the best test, and the best guarantee, of quality is competition and comparison.

Private Prisons
Are Cost Effective

by Wayne Calabrese

About the author: *Wayne Calabrese is president of Wackenhut Corrections Corporation, a private prison firm.*

Editor's note: This viewpoint is adapted from testimony Wayne Calabrese gave before the Little Hoover Commission Public Hearing on Prison Issues in Sacramento, California, on August 28, 1997.

Mr. Chairman, members of the Commission, thank you for the opportunity to appear today to address the issue of prison privatization. My name is Wayne Calabrese; I am president of Wackenhut Corrections Corporation, with principal offices in Palm Beach Gardens, Florida.

The contracting out of the integrated design, financing, construction and operation of a correctional facility to the private sector began in the early 1980s. In 1997 there are more than 135 facilities and 85,000 prisoner places under private sector operation or construction around the world.

With 37 contracts in the United States, Canada, Puerto Rico, England and Australia, and over 26,000 prisoner places under contract, Wackenhut Corrections is a recognized leader in the private development and operation of correctional facilities, with approximately 30% of the total worldwide market.

Prison construction is a growth industry in this country and the cost is enormous. Per cell construction costs range from $20,000 to $40,000, and the annual operational costs can easily exceed the annual cost of attending a prestigious private university.

But the cost of allowing a career criminal to remain on the street, including the cost of additional police, insurance losses, and direct financial loss to victims, has been estimated to exceed one-half million dollars per year. Add to this the immeasurable cost of our loss of personal safety and security, and our investment in the infrastructure of our prisons begins to make fundamental, good sense.

Reprinted, with permission, from Wayne Calabrese, testimony before the Little Hoover Commission Public Hearing on Prison Issues, Sacramento, California, August 28, 1997, published at www.securitymanagement.com/library/private.html.

But as this Commission and its members are only too aware, the demand for public service is not always matched by public resources. In the face of ever-greater demands upon fewer and fewer tax dollars, the public sector has looked increasingly to public-private partnerships to deliver mandated services.

Mr. Chairman, members of the Committee, prison privatization is not an experiment; it is not a "pilot project." Governments throughout the United States and around the world are achieving real cost savings in the development and operation of prisons by the private sector. Indeed, the United States Bureau of Prisons, widely viewed as one of the pre-eminent correctional organizations in

> *"The elimination of a single unnecessary 24-hour officer post can result in annual savings of nearly $150,000–$200,000 based upon wages and benefits."*

the world, recognized the value of public-private partnering in its recent contract award of the operations of the 2,048-bed Taft, California, federal institution to Wackenhut Corrections.

Public-private prison partnerships can lead to:

- reduction of construction costs by 25–40%
- reduction of operational costs, which account for more than 80% of a prison's life-cycle costs, by 10–20%
- acceleration of facility construction by as much as 30–50%
- assured high quality service
- budget certainty

It is critical, however, to understand the methods employed by the private sector in achieving these results and to carefully address the issues which inevitably arise when public sector policy objectives and private sector shareholder interests are brought face-to-face in a public-private partnership. Through the application of careful planning and drafting, privatization contracts can successfully marry public sector ends with private sector means, ensuring a "win-win" result for public and private sector participants alike.

Methods Used by Private Companies

There are three primary areas for cost-savings by the private sector in the construction and operation of a correctional facility:

- efficient facility design
- fast-track, firm-fixed-price, design/build methods
- private sector management practices

Efficient Facility Design. Most savings in the construction and operation of a correctional facility flow directly from the facility's design. Typically, states design a facility through "committee consensus." It is not unusual for a state to have a correctional facility designed through the combined efforts of representatives of public works, treasury, legal, and corrections, working under the direction of design and construction consultants who have produced or at least studied facilities designed by prior committees. The result, predictably, is an over-designed, operationally inefficient and costly facility, plagued by change-orders and finger-pointing, and a resolve to improve the make-up and procedures of the committee before the next facility is designed.

Private sector designs begin and end with operational efficiency honed by competition. The public sector sets the design and operational standards, generally by reference to established standards such as those published by the American Correctional Association (ACA) or an analogous state regulatory agency. The private sector develops a design which meets these standards and incorporates the operational imperatives of the private operator. In other words, the facility's form follows the facility's function, a desirable result often reversed by committee protocols.

While an efficient design can save significant dollars in construction costs, generally estimated in the range of 2,540% of comparable public sector construction costs, the real savings over time are in operations. Facility construction costs generally amount to no more than 15% of the lifecycle costs of a facility; at least 85–90% of the facility's lifecycle costs are operational, and at least 65–70% of the operational costs are staff-related.

For example, the elimination of a single unnecessary 24-hour officer post can result in annual savings of nearly $150,000–$200,000 based upon wages and benefits. Clearly, a facility design which achieves operational efficiency through an elimination of redundant posts, while maintaining or improving operational integrity, is a design which will produce significant, long-term savings.

Fast-Track, Firm-Fixed-Price, Design/Build Methods. It is not unusual for a state to take three to five years to design and construct a correctional facility. The private sector will generally deliver a prison within 12–18 months of a notice to proceed through the use of fast-track, design/build methods. For every $100 million of facility construction, this shortened completion cycle results in at least $15 million in savings through reduced capitalized interest expenses, alone.

More importantly, private sector firm-fixed-price, design/build contracts result in the elimination of change-order costs which are a regular feature of almost every public sector construction project. Public sector construction procurement requirements virtually ensure cost overruns and broken completion schedules; indeed, most public procurement methods "incentivize" such results by paying a fee to the architect who certifies the need for a change-order based upon a percentage of the submitted change order cost. By placing the risk of such costs and delays on the private contractor through completion bonds and liquidated damages, and eliminating the opportunity for change orders through firm, fixed-price contracts, private sector methods virtually ensure on-budget and timely completion of projects.

Private Sector Management Practices. By applying private sector management practices to such areas as abuse of overtime and sick time, and procurement of goods and services, the private sector can generally realize significant savings in on-going operating costs without sacrificing either the quality or quantity of required correctional services.

Measures for Ensuring Quality and Professionalism

There are at least seven measures which can be utilized to ensure quality and professionalism in private correctional services:

1. the terms of the contract
2. a facility-based monitor
3. annual government audits
4. in-house corporate auditing
5. accreditation systems
6. competition among private operators
7. media scrutiny

> *"A healthy respect for a vigilant media is a powerful guarantee of private operator accountability."*

I will comment briefly on each of these measures.

Contract Terms. A carefully drafted contract is the single most effective measure for ensuring high quality and professionalism in private sector correctional services. The terms of every private operational contract require the operator to meet, and in some cases exceed, all performance standards, laws, regulations and rules applicable to the public sector. Breach of these standards can result in contract sanctions, including loss of revenue and contract termination. Over the years, many well-drafted, thorough contracts have been developed which have served states well in establishing a responsive client/contractor relationship with private sector companies. Indeed, Wackenhut's contract with California's Corrections Department for our McFarland Community Corrections Facility has proved quite durable and effective for both parties.

Government Monitor. Most contracts call for an on-site public sector monitor who has complete and unrestricted access, at all times, to all facility employees, prisoners, records and information, and who is directly responsible for audited company performance on a daily basis. This is almost never true of a public facility.

Annual Government Audits. It is common for the government to perform an annual audit of contract performance. Some contracts today tie performance to remuneration through a system of performance-linked payments.

In-House Audits. Private companies employ in-house corporate personnel to monitor and audit all aspects of operational performance. Wackenhut's corporate personnel monitor such matters as security incident reports, health services, overtime and sick-time, and facility purchases on a daily, weekly and monthly basis.

Accreditation. In addition to government and in-house monitors and auditors, most contracts call for accreditation of operations within one or two years of opening by such third-party accreditation agencies as the American Correctional Association (ACH) and the National Commission on Correctional Health Care (NCCHC).

These accreditation systems serve as an outside and objective quality assurance program. Wackenhut has achieved, or is in the process of obtaining ACA and NCCHC accreditation for all of its domestic facilities.

Competition. There is a healthy competition among private correctional service providers which results in the need for each to maintain a standard of performance consistent with a marketable reputation and something as fundamental and perhaps quaint as the notion of "pride." At Wackenhut we consider our reputation to be our single most important marketing asset; the word "adequate" is never used in-house as a synonym for "satisfactory."

> *"A prison designed by a private sector operator is the best guarantee of a prison designed to maximize safety, security and cost-efficiency."*

Media Scrutiny. We are all familiar with most of our public institutions—we have all spent time in schools, libraries, and hospitals. But for most of us, our prisons remain hidden behind a shroud of movie images and sensational news stories, and we are naturally curious about an institution that is financed by all but seen by few.

Add to this natural curiosity the fact that the operation of a prison by a private company is still a relatively novel idea and you readily appreciate the media's heightened focus on privately operated prisons.

Private operators have come to understand and to expect that an otherwise uneventful incident in a publicly operated prison will generate significant media interest and coverage in a privately operated facility. A healthy respect for a vigilant media is a powerful guarantee of private operator accountability.

Potential Problems Can Be Overcome

Critics of privatization often raise issues regarding the appropriateness of involving the private sector in our prison system and the perceived tendency of a profit motive to erode the quality of service delivered by the private sector to governments at the local, state, and federal level. . . .

Those who suggest that a private contract service provider will make a profit by underpaying its employees, or cutting back on the quality of prisoner services and programs betray a fundamental misunderstanding of the nature of a service company and its relationship to its customers, as well as a flawed concept of how a service company makes money.

Paying employees in a labor-intensive service industry less than competitive wages and benefits inevitably results in a dissatisfied workforce and a high rate of attrition. Each correctional officer represents a significant investment of time and money by a private operator. A high rate of staff turnover means substantial operating losses, as well as operational inefficiency associated with lack of employee continuity and loss of experience-linked productivity.

The quality of prisoner rehabilitation programs is frequently the means by which the private operator distinguishes its service from that of the public sector. Professional and effective prisoner programs result in a safe, secure and ordered routine, the foundation of cost-effectiveness in any prison operation.

As previously discussed, a prison designed by a private sector operator is the best guarantee of a prison designed to maximize safety, security and cost-efficiency. Wackenhut employs four in-house architects to guarantee the safety, security and cost-efficiency of all of our facility conceptual designs.

The issue of private companies lobbying for laws that increase prison populations in order to maintain population-linked revenues overlooks the fact that prison populations have been increasing nationally at a uniformly high rate of growth with little or no influence from a private sector which has less than 4% of all prison beds under contract in the United States. An equally compelling but incorrect case for such inappropriate lobbying could be made against public sector unions or other public sector interest groups motivated by a desire to increase or at least maintain public sector jobs and benefits. Unfortunately for society on the whole, criminal population projections would appear to require little or no assistance from private or public sector interest groups into the foreseeable future.

The concept of profit is worthy of further consideration. I worked for years in the public sector. I never once attended a government budget meeting where a department representative reported a failure to spend all of last year's allocated budget and sought a reduced budget for the next year.

To be sure, many public sector agencies operate efficiently. But public sector efficiencies which in the private sector would result in profits are, in the public sector, generally absorbed in growth—growth in staff, growth in procurements, and growth in bureaucracy.

Despite the best efforts of governments around the world to emulate private sector methods through a variety of means, more than marginal savings frequently seem unobtainable or unsustainable. I suspect this is due to the lack of a profit based structure. In short, no one has yet devised a better pencil sharpener than the private sector in open competition.

> *"Despite the best efforts of governments around the world to emulate private sector methods . . . more than marginal savings frequently seem unobtainable."*

I want to thank you, Mr. Chairman, and members of the Commission, for the opportunity to address these important issues as you consider the utilization of privatization as a means of achieving the State's correctional objectives.

Private Prisons Provide More Incentive for Rehabilitation

by Abigail McCarthy

About the author: *Abigail McCarthy is a writer and frequent contributor to* Commonweal *magazine, an independent journal of opinion edited and managed by lay Catholics.*

As the crime bill swung into its second round the summer of 1994, vacationers with whom I was sharing Cape Cod tended to grow nostalgic about the relatively crime-free times of their youth. I, too, thought fondly of the days when we put the key on the ledge over the front door—if we locked the door at all—and the only crimes that fretted our parents were kids swiping melons from nearby farmers' fields or, once or twice, some petty embezzlement by a hard-pressed employee in one of the town's businesses.

Oh, we were aware of big crime. In his time Jesse James and his gang had robbed a bank in a town not far away and, during my adolescence, Al Capone reigned in Chicago and often popped up in the headlines. But in Minnesota we did not live with crime as an inescapable fact of life.

Now, living as I do in Washington, D.C., where homicide is commonplace and teen-agers carry assault weapons as ordinary gear, I take crime as a given. I suppose it speaks to the adaptability of human nature. I am, I realize, fortunate that I have known personally only one person who was shot—and that not fatally, although the intent to kill was there. (She had failed to let go her purse easily when it was grabbed.)

Crime Is Commonplace

But threatening incidents are commonplace. For example, a neighbor was attacked and pursued at dusk on the way from her parking space to our building—right past two supposedly guarded embassies. And someone jumped out of the shubbery and waylaid a passing woman, holding her at knife-point on our front steps until she yielded her wallet, bank card, and pin number. (Our sentimental doorman said that he assumed that they were lovers!) And things like this happen on an almost weekly basis.

When I go out to take a walk or to go down the street to the dentist or the bookstore I automatically de-mug myself. I put my keys, one credit card, some cash, and my driver's license (for identification) in a pocket—an inside one, if possible. I carry a purse with some money in it to mollify any purse-snatcher who might be enraged to find it empty. I also keep several quarters in one hand to placate the more aggressive panhandlers who wave paper cups under my nose. (On the same principle a friend of mine keeps a purse with money visible in her front hall.) I walk fast looking straight ahead. Eye contact, I have read, is often interpreted as "dissing" or showing disrespect to young gang members. Lest readers get the wrong idea, I hasten to add that I find this necessary in one of the best sections of our capital city.

Should I and my friends not then rejoice in the passage of a crime bill that is intended to take our potential assailants off the street, increase the number of police and prisons, and make certain that repeating violent offenders will spend their lives behind bars? Not really.

> *"Most states have a sorry record in the administration of prisons."*

First of all, hard as it may be for my frightened contemporaries to believe, we older women are the least likely victims of violent crime despite the prevalence of incidents like those I have described above. A poll taken in the summer of 1994 by *Money* magazine established that fact and the correlative one that the most likely victims are African-American males between the ages of twelve and nineteen. What will make us safer and release us more surely from the prison of fear are the rehabilitation of those young and violent who are now offenders, and measures to prevent others from joining them. It seems that the building of the additional prisons for which the crime bill will provide the money will do little or nothing for either deterrence or rehabilitation.

Failures of the State Prison System

First of all, prisons, once built, must be staffed and maintained. Local jurisdictions simply do not have the money to do more than they are now doing for their overcrowded facilities. Secondly, most states have a sorry record in the administration of prisons. Take only one lurid example. In a state as supposedly enlightened as Massachusetts a woman prisoner named Joan Andrade died this month because the infectious pneumonia from which she was suffering went undiagnosed and untreated for ten days. Three other inmates of the same women's prison died under similar circumstances in 1992. According to the *Boston Globe,* the State Department of Correction's supervision of the health provider had been shockingly inadequate. Less shocking than death by neglect but also an indictment of prison administration is that it is almost taken for granted that a young man entering prison is entering a school for crime. "I am a career criminal," said Ernest Anderson, talking to Anthony Ramirez of the *New York Times* (August 14, 1994) and detailing a decade of his life spent in five different prisons.

> *"There is a rich irony in the fact that the profit motive makes better rehabilitation than does state social policy."*

But in Ernest Anderson's story there is a ray of hope emanating from an unlikely source: privately run prisons. In the facility in which he is now held, the Metro-Davidson Facility in Nashville, Tennessee, Anderson says he has been able to turn his life around. "The private prison industry has no shortage of critics," writes Ramirez, "from public sector unions out to protect their jobs to civil liberty advocates who warn that company-run prisons are less accountable." Yet in the thirteen states in which privately run prisons are allowed, the larger correction services are demonstrating that providing ample prison services cuts costs and is productive of rehabilitation for the inmates.

Profit and Rehabilitation

Private correction officials and wardens say that the gain for the companies comes from changing the unhealthy environment found in so many prisons. "At Corrections Corporation prisons you don't have the atmosphere of impending violence that you have in a state prison," says William C. La Rowe, director of a Texas prisoners' rights group. Part of the formula used to improve the prison atmosphere is to keep potentially quarrelsome prisoners like Ernest Anderson so busy with drug rehabilitation, recreational and educational programs that trouble will not tempt them. At Metro-Davidson inmates can get a high school equivalency degree and attend programs that teach marketable skills as well as take a six-month psychological counseling course designed to bring brooding loners out of isolation.

Perhaps there is a rich irony in the fact that the profit motive makes better rehabilitation than does state social policy. The welfare and safety of prisoners turn out to be good business. It is possible that, until there is another crime bill with strong preventive programs, prevention of crime will also become the province of far-sighted entrepreneurs. And hopeless youths will have futures and our communities will be safe once again.

Providing Financial Incentives for Incarceration Is Unethical

by C. Stone Brown

About the author: *C. Stone Brown is a Black history/political writer who resides in Philadelphia.*

The United States of America has quietly become one of the world's leaders in the rate of incarcerating its citizens. Federal and state prisons have reached the dubious milestone of having a million or more inmates in prison. That number does not even count America's jail population, which according to the U.S. Justice Department is a record 490,442, double the jail population in the 1980s.

The custodians of America's penal systems have abandoned the idea of rehabilitating convicts. No doubt, the custodians are acting on orders from an impatient mainstream America, who regard criminals (with exception to white collar criminals) to be innately corrupt, natural born predators of society.

What is America's collective sociological need that drives its approach to dealing with crime? Statistically, violent crime disproportionately affects the underprivileged of our society. However, solutions are not often the ideas of the underprivileged, frequently they are paternally administered by the privileged class. If the solution to America's crime problem is left to the actions of the privileged class, we should expect the solution to augment their status, while further alienating the underprivileged. This explains the presence of America's growing "Prison Industry." According to the *National Prison Project Journal,* some of America's largest Wall Street brokerage firms, such as Goldman Sachs & Co., Prudential Insurance Co., Smith Barney Shearson, Inc., and Merrill Lynch & Co., are underwriting prison construction with private tax-exempt bonds. Indeed, America has found its antidote to crime, it is Wall Street's biggest merger to date—crime and capitalism.

Reprinted, with permission, from "Crime, Capitalism, and Black America," by C. Stone Brown, Z *Magazine*, October 1995.

Does Crime Pay?

Crime and capitalism is a very suggestive expression; it immediately discloses an American trend—that crime does pay, and if justice does not prevail, profits surely will. The increasing number of private prison firms are the latest societal indicator that "street" crime is permissible, under the tacit prescription that it is contained, managed and operated like a business enterprise.

Private prison firms are very attractive to many states whose budgets have been depleted by mandatory sentencing guidelines and the latest "three strikes you're out" craze. These private firms offer their services on a per diem charge to house the state's convicts. This relieves state governments of the burdensome cost of constructing new prisons, paying guard wages, insurance, pensions, and other associated maintenance security cost.

There are approximately 50,000 private prison beds in the United States; experts believe this number will rise considerably in the next decade. According to an article in the *Toronto Star,* the largest private prison company is Corrections Corporation of America (CCA). CCA was founded in 1983 by Doctor Crants, a graduate of West Point and Harvard Business School.

CCA is listed on the prestigious New York Stock Exchange, it answers to shareholders and has board meetings like all publicly traded companies. What does distinguish CCA from other listed companies is how crime affects stockholder profits. Indeed, the annual FBI and Justice Department national crime data, are excellent leading indicators of future dividends. For companies like CCA, the local Metro sections of American newspapers are no less important than the business section.

CCA has grown considerably since its debut in 1983. It is now a $100-million company with 21 prisons spread over America, Australia, and the United Kingdom. CCA has already come under scrutiny in two states. Tennessee's $60 million contract with CCA is currently under review by the state legislature, and at two of their private facilities in Texas, a 1990 report revealed that "inexperienced" prison employees had used excessive force on inmates. Additionally, inmates were not extended services which were required under the state contract to assist inmates' return to society. Few would argue, it is in the interest of CCA profits, that prisoners return to their facility and not back into society.

> *"Crime does pay, and if justice does not prevail, profits surely will."*

Surprisingly, some of America's icon companies are diversifying their investments in private prison construction. For instance, American Express has invested millions in private prison construction in Oklahoma. And General Electric (GE) has invested in "life" sentences by financing private prison construction in Tennessee.

Chapter 3

The Prisoner as a Commodity

As America's system of justice sanctions the profits and privatization of prisons, convicted criminals are no longer viewed as pariahs of society. Comparable to slaves during America's colonial period, convicts have become a very desirable commodity across the nation. Perhaps the convicts are not as seductive as the profits they yield to many communities. For example, the state of North Carolina sends its convicts to a private prison in Oklahoma, and recently the state of Virginia chartered 150 inmates to a county-owned, for-profit detention center in east Texas. In 31 days, those 150 Virginia prisoners earned the Texas county more than $200,000. The owner of the east Texas detention center, Bobby Ross, remarked: "It's kind of like a factory in a sense."

For many involved in the industry of crime, it's no surprise that a county in

> *"Convicts have become a very desirable commodity across the nation."*

Texas would be one of the first to recognize the profitable merging of crime and capitalism. It is projected that in just a few months, Texas will have the largest penal system in the country, larger than even the federal government. At a projected figure of 155,000 inmates, Texas knows convicts like Idaho knows potatoes.

Although Texas may be the Lone Star State, they have plenty of company when it comes to taking advantage of America's swelling prison population. In California, crime is a synonym for job security. Just ask the state correctional officers whose average salary is $45,000 annually. It was a small investment for the prison guard union to contribute nearly a half million dollars ($425,000) to Governor Pete Wilson's gubernatorial campaign. This was the largest single contribution ever reported by a candidate for governor. If the old adage "money talks," has any legitimacy, one can only deduce that Governor Pete Wilson was being advised in unequivocal terms that "crime" is the commerce of California's future.

In the East, New York city crime is a "cash cow" for one particular Republican county in New York state. According to the state's corrections committee chair, in 1992, the 110th district received $124 million in salaries, local purchases of food and supplies, maintenance contracts and other operating expenses. Suburban counties similar to the 110th district in New York state have a financial interest in watching urban crime flourish across the nation. For instance, in New York state, 71 percent of prison inmates are from New York city. However, nearly 99 percent of those prisoners are transported upstate to New York's affluent white middle class suburbs, where urban crime is converted to good paying jobs.

In Pennsylvania, privatization of prisons is being challenged in court by the Prison Employees Union. According to an August 22, 1995, *Philadelphia In-*

quirer article: "Prison Union Sues Over Loss of Jobs," caught between a bitter law suit is the second largest private prison company, Wackenhut Corrections Corporation. The lawsuit was filed by the Delaware County prison employees union, asserting the county's decision to privatize was illegal under the state constitution. With 250 union employees, the union has no assurances of being rehired by Wackenhut. With only one labor union in its 23 U.S. locations, Wackenhut isn't exactly a haven for union activity. In other areas of the state, draconian measures are being employed to help defray the cost of incarcerating inmates. For instance, counties such as Berks, Chester, Montgomery, and Lehigh charge inmates for health care and in some instances rent, says Angus Love, executive director of Pennsylvania Institutional Law Project, a legal service agency. When inmates are unable to pay, collection agencies are hired to pursue payment. Critics see such measures as an unnecessary roadblock to financially handicap a convict's chance to integrate back into society.

> *"When the privileged of society take aim to profit from the misery of crime, they become accomplice to social disorder, complicit in creating a criminal class."*

A Slave-Like Work Force

Along with warehousing criminals, state penal systems have located another method of exploiting its prison population. State governments are instituting a slave-like work force within its prison walls. With cooperative agreements with small manufacturing companies, states are merging in creating a semi-factory prison work force. The prison work force is paid minimum wage, at least where labor unions have forced their hand. Inmates net approximately $1 an hour after deductions. Thirty states have legalized privately run operations. Here are just a few of the states, companies and products/services involved:

- California: logos for Lexus automobiles
- Hawaii: packing Spaulding golf balls
- Maryland: modular houses, processed hot dogs
- New Mexico: hotel chain reservations
- Oregon: designer blue jeans, called "prison blues"
- South Carolina: electronic cables
- Washington: Eddie Bauer garments

There is also a boom in companies vending their product or services to the "prison industry." How many industries can boast the rate of its target market (prison population) is growing 8.5 percent annually? The scope of vendors at the 1995 (ACA) American Correctional Association Convention, range from a Dial soap representative, to QueTel Corporation, who impressed prison wardens with technology to bar code inmates.

Should Americans be legitimately fearful that Wall Street has recognized that crime not only pays, but it pays billions? Ask Arthur McDonald, former owner of California's largest private prison firm, Eclectic Communications, Incorporated. McDonald, now retired from the $10 million sale of Eclectic, told the *Los Angeles Times,* "Crime pays. I hate saying that, but it really does." Since that sale in 1988, Eclectic has received contracts exceeding $50 million.

Profits Instead of Justice

Have we reached that critical stage in America where the alienated and disenfranchised of our society are valued only for their eventual imprisonment? Although these are questions for all Americans to answer, how they are answered, will disproportionately affect the future of African Americans.

The American prison and jail population is over 1.5 million. While African Americans are 13 percent of the general population, they are nearly half of the 1.5 million incarcerated population. Experts believe that the prison population has swelled due to the so-called "War on Drugs." Drug related convictions are certainly one of the reasons African Americans are disproportionately incarcerated, but one has to question why? According to the Department of Health and Human Services, 2.4 million (64.4 percent) of crack users are White, compared to 1 million Blacks (26.6 percent). Yet, in a 1992 study by the U.S. Sentencing Commission, 91.3 percent of those sentenced for federal crack offenses were Black, while 3 percent were White. Such stark numbers reveal that African Americans are the flesh that maintains a profitable "prison industry."

When the privileged of society take aim to profit from the misery of crime, they become accomplice to social disorder, complicit in creating a criminal class. Their quality of life becomes tied to a misery/revenue index where profits are merely a function of the misery of others. America's symbol of justice is unfolding before our eyes. It is no longer a blind-folded woman, it is now an accountant, not balancing the scales of justice, but debits and credits on a balance sheet.

Private Prisons
Foster Corruption

by Vince Beiser

About the author: *Vince Beiser is a New York City–based journalist who writes frequently on prison issues.*

Want a hot stock tip? Get into prisons. Privately operated, for-profit prisons are multiplying like mushrooms all across the United States. The companies that run them have become Wall Street darlings, and with good reason.

The first private prison opened for business in 1983, holding a mere 350 inmates. Today, almost 90,000 inmates languish in over 100 for-profit lockups in the United States and Puerto Rico. With an increasing number of states considering legislation to allow private prisons to operate, and thousands of projected prison beds already contracted out to private companies, the industry is set to sustain its dizzying expansion. Financial analysts predict that private prisons will house as many as 400,000 by 2006. "This growth would be considered phenomenal in any other consumer-related industry," notes a typical report by Rodman and Renshaw, an equity research firm.

However good it is for shareholders, though, this explosive growth carries disturbing implications for the criminal justice system. An industry whose raw materials are incarcerated human beings has every reason to support policies that get more and more Americans thrown in jail for longer and longer sentences, regardless of their objective merits.

Escalating Profits

As it is, the boom in the private prison industry echoes that in America's prison population. Owing to massive increases in drug arrests and "three strikes and you're out" mandatory sentencing laws, the number of people confined in local, state and Federal correctional institutions has more than tripled since 1980, to over 1.6 million today. Scrambling to cope with overcrowding and escalating costs, and encouraged by the "privatize everything" climate in Washington, policy makers are turning increasingly to privately run prisons—which

Reprinted, with permission, from "Jailing for Dollars," by Vince Beiser, *New Leader*, May 5, 1997.

claim to run more cheaply and efficiently.

The result has been a bonanza for private prison companies. The largest of these, controlling nearly half the market, is the Corrections Corporation of America (CCA). Its revenues have soared from $152 million in 1994 to $293 million in 1996, when its profits reached a record $30 million. CCA's main competitor, Wackenhut Corrections Corporation (WCC), saw its profits nearly double last year on revenues of over $137 million. And WCC's 1997 first quarter earnings are up 75 per cent over last year's. An exuber-

> *"[Private prisons] might not be saving any taxpayer money at all."*

ant WCC launched a subsidiary to build its prisons. Even the smaller fish have joined the feeding frenzy; revenues at Cornell Corrections, for instance, more than doubled in '96 to top $13 million.

Small wonder the industry leaders have earned "buy" recommendations from a bevy of investment analysts, including Lazard Frères. The industry has spawned its own symbiotic class of lobbyists, academics, consultants, investment analysts, and financiers. Smith Barney, Prudential Securities and other top financial institutions have been financing private prison construction. The Texas firm of Raucher, Pierce and Refsnes rakes in several million dollars annually by buying and reselling private-prison-issued bonds and securities.

So what could be wrong with private prison companies and their friends making money by providing a service more cheaply than the government can? For a start, they might not be saving any taxpayer money at all. While a few studies have found that some private prisons operate more cheaply than their public counterparts, others have found them to cost the same or more. A comprehensive General Accounting Office report issued in August "could not conclude whether privatization saved money."

A reason may be that private prisons generate hidden costs. By law, nearly all must be monitored by state bureaucrats, whose salaries are not counted in their operating costs. Furthermore, many of their inmates are less dangerous offenders who require less supervision.

A Conflict of Interest

One of the ways private prisons do end up saving money is by relying almost exclusively on nonunion workers, who generally receive lower salaries and fewer benefits than their unionized, public-sector counterparts. Some companies offer stock options in lieu of a pension plan. But since companies are compensated by the government on a per-prisoner per-day basis, the potential for abuse is built in. "If a guard knows his bonus depends on the amount of money the prison makes," observes American University law professor Ira Robbins, "he has every incentive not to write up inmates for good behavior that will get them released sooner."

Most ominous, according to Steven Donziger, editor of the book, *The Real War on Crime*, "is that it all creates a whole power base to push for continuing to expand the prison population as a source of economic profit, regardless of whether that's a good thing for society." Spending on prisons has topped $20 billion a year and continues to grow, even as government spending on health care, education and just about every other social service is being slashed. In California, for instance, since 1980 the percentage of the state budget devoted to education has dropped 35 per cent; appropriations for prisons, meanwhile, have risen five-fold. Prison construction is draining resources from other needed services, and strict sentencing laws have put many more people behind bars; but there is no clear evidence that any of this is having a significant effect on crime rates.

Nonetheless, the powerful California prison guards' union has already proved that an economic interest group will gladly lobby for more prisoners. The union has also contributed well over $1 million to Governor Pete Wilson, a staunch crime hawk. And in 1994, it spent tens of thousands of dollars backing the "three strikes" voter initiative mandating longer sentences for repeat offenders. More prisoners mean more jobs for prison guards.

> *"Private prison companies have an . . . economic incentive to support longer sentences."*

Private prison companies have an identical economic incentive to support longer sentences, reducing parole and, of course, more prison construction. With that in mind, it's disturbing to note that as their profits have ballooned, so have their political contributions.

According to Federal Election Commission filings, total contributions to candidates for Federal office from private prison companies, their top executives and their spouses rose from $27,200 in 1992 to $147,650 in 1996. Additional cash is handed out at the state level. In Florida, for instance, which has more private prisons than any other state besides Texas, WCC's campaign contributions went from zero in 1994 to $28,500 in 1996. Doctor R. Crants, CEO of the Tennessee-based CCA, also chipped in $5,000 to the Florida Republican Party, and another $1,000 to the Florida Democrats for good measure. The figures aren't huge, yet, but the trend is clear. "Until very recently, we were only in half a dozen states," says WCC Chief Executive Officer George C. Zoley. "Now we're doubling that, and as we continue to expand into other states we will make more contributions."

No Need for Lobbying

So far, private prison company money is not explicitly aimed at supporting tough-on-crime legislation—mainly because it doesn't need to be. Company executives say that at this point they have no need to push explicitly for harsher sentencing laws because politicians across the spectrum are already falling all over themselves to do it for them. "We have never been involved in lobbying for such laws," says Zoley. "It's completely unnecessary. There's so much support already for tougher laws."

Prison companies are thus free to spend their money on supporting lawmakers who want to use private facilities to hold all those new prisoners they are keen to lock up, and on convincing others to get on board. Only about 30 states so far allow private prisons to operate; CCA and WCC retain professional lobbyists in many of the states that are considering following suit. Momentum is clearly building on their side. President Clinton himself is pushing for the federal government to contract out more to private prison companies, which may explain why Crants and his wife donated $2,000 to his last campaign.

Having powerful connections also helps. WCC's board includes a former director of the Federal Bureau of Prisons, Carter-era Attorney General Benjamin Civiletti and a former governor of Illinois. And the board of its parent, the Wackenhut Corporation, has included such heavies as Reagan-era National Security Adviser Frank Carlucci, ex-CIA director William Rayborn and ex-deputy director Bobby Ray Inman.

For its part, in addition to a board that includes another former Federal Bureau of Prisons director, CCA enjoys excellent ties with the political and business elite of its home state. Co-founder Thomas Beasley once chaired the Tennessee Republican Party, and is especially tight with Governor Don Sundquist. The two started a successful barbecue restaurant chain together in 1988, and Beasley has contributed over $16,000 to Sundquist's campaigns since 1993. Sundquist's chief of staff owns CCA stock, and his main adviser on prison expansion is a former CCA lobbyist. Little wonder, then, that the governor backed CCA's efforts to open a new prison in Tennessee last year over the objections of the state comptroller.

Buoyed by the swelling tide of new prisoners, private prisons seem certain to continue their stunning rise. What may get drowned in the process is a criminal justice system that works primarily for the good of society.

Private Prisons Are Abusive and Inefficient

by Eric Bates

About the author: *Eric Bates is a staff writer for the* Independent, *an alternative weekly in Durham, North Carolina.*

James Neal is a short, muscular man with close-cropped hair who has spent the past twelve years behind bars for armed robbery. He is also one of the most valuable commodities to trade hands in Youngstown, Ohio, since the steel industry abandoned the city more than a decade ago. In 1997 Neal was among the first "loads" of inmates bused from the District of Columbia to a new prison run by Corrections Corporation of America (CCA), the world's largest operator of for-profit lockups. CCA stood to make $182 million guarding the prisoners, and Youngstown-area residents lined up to apply for hundreds of jobs with the company. Those who toured the prison before it opened were assured they need not worry about the supply of out-of-state inmates. "If one of them dies," a company tour guide said, "they'll send another one."

Mistreatment at Youngstown

The day after Neal arrived, a few of his fellow prisoners argued with guards about their treatment. Although the warden later admitted that no one was in danger and no property was threatened, CCA responded to the inmate complaints by dropping canisters of tear gas designed for outdoor use into four cellblocks. As hundreds of blinded and choking prisoners gasped for air, a team of black-uniformed officers in full riot gear known as the "Goon Squad" handcuffed them, beat them and sprayed them in the face with Mace. "It was kind of like a war atmosphere," says Neal, wearing a dark-green prison uniform. "You could hear the canisters whistling down and exploding—whump! No life or limb or property was at stake. CCA just overreacted. I thought, 'Damn, they could have killed me.'"

The excessive use of force proved to be a prelude to stark mistreatment at Youngstown. The medium-security prison was actually taking many maximum-

Reprinted, with permission, from "CCA, the Sequel," by Eric Bates, *The Nation*, June 7, 1999.

security inmates, and the inexperienced CCA guards were ill prepared to handle the volatile mix. More than twenty prisoners were stabbed in the first ten months, and two died from their wounds. At least seven inmates died from medical conditions, and the company's own audit showed that the prison provided inadequate care to hundreds of prisoners. After Neal and other prisoners filed a class-action lawsuit over substandard treatment and excessive force, CCA once again ordered the riot squad into the cellblocks, forcing inmates to strip, parade naked in front of female staff and lie on the concrete floors for hours while their cells were searched. "I felt like I was on a slave ship," Neal recalls. "I never felt anything so humiliating in my entire life!"

> *"The lack of training for guards and the lack of programs for inmates in private prisons exacerbate violence."*

Public officials paid scant attention to the abuse of prisoners, however, until the danger began spilling over the razor-wire fence surrounding the prison. In July 1998 six inmates escaped in broad daylight by cutting through the fence—a technique they had routinely practiced in front of guards, snipping the wire to trip the alarms and then running back into crowds of inmates playing softball on a nearby field. After the breakout Ohio Governor George Voinovich called for the prison to be closed and Attorney General Janet Reno ordered a federal investigation.

The abuses at Youngstown are scarcely isolated incidents. Since January, 1998, the company has experienced more than its share of prisoner escapes and brutality by guards. Coming so close together, the repeated misconduct underscores the way private prisons cut corners at the expense of workers, prisoners and the public.

Escalating Violence

The lack of training for guards and the lack of programs for inmates in private prisons exacerbate violence. In Tennessee a prisoner transferred from Youngstown was stabbed and killed in August 1998 by another inmate shipped from Ohio. At another prison in Tennessee, CCA covered up abuses of inmates transported from Wisconsin, who were thrown against walls and zapped with stun guns. Eight company employees, including the security chief, were fired after the incident became public. In New Jersey the company improperly restrained and forcibly sedated immigrants awaiting hearings; in Arizona inmates demonstrated at a CCA prison to protest the lack of recreational and educational programs.

Lax security at CCA prisons across the country has enabled an unusually high number of escapes. At the company's South Central prison in Tennessee, four prisoners cut through a fence in October 1998 with a bolt cutter they received in the mail; a guard who heard the alarm simply shut it off without investigating.

In January 1999, a convicted killer walked out through the gates dressed in a guard's uniform given to him by a female employee. A Cuban immigrant over-powered a guard and fled from a CCA lockup in Houston, and a convicted killer in a DC jail run by the company climbed out a window undetected before falling eight floors to his death. Guards did not even notice anything amiss when an unidentified woman loaded the inmate's body into her car and drove him to a hospital.

Such an inability to handle the most basic function of a prison—keeping prisoners behind bars—seems to suggest that private companies are scarcely the efficient and reliable jailers they claim to be. After fifteen years of privatization, officials still have almost no reliable data to assess whether for-profit prisons are doing their job—or living up to their promise to save taxpayers money. "Only a few of the more than a hundred privately operated facilities in existence have been studied," a federal report concluded in October 1998, "and these studies do not offer compelling evidence of superiority."

A Growing Industry

The lack of evidence hasn't stopped public officials from turning to private prisons like CCA. The company added more than 18,000 beds last year, thanks in no small part to its generosity. In Wisconsin, which has shipped more than 2,100 inmates to CCA prisons, the governor and six key legislators received $4,000 in campaign contributions from company chairman Doctor R. Crants. In Ohio, the governor's brother received the contract to build the CCA prison in Youngstown.

Such friends in high places have helped CCA profit handsomely from crime. Net income for the first nine months of 1998 topped $60 million, up 63 percent from 1997. In April 1998 the company bought US Corrections Corporation, its second-largest rival, further securing its hold on the industry. But as competition declines, officials warn, so does the incentive for private prisons to offer competitive contracts. "CCA is so overwhelmingly bigger than everybody else, they'll win hands down," says Russell Boraas, who oversees private prisons for Virginia. "That's not good for the industry, and that's not good for taxpayers."

In reality, "CCA" now exists only as a brand name. The company stopped trading on the stock market in January, when it "merged" with a real estate trust it had formed. Prison Realty Corporation essentially operates as a tax shelter, enabling the company to evade paying any corporate income taxes. Under the arrangement, the trust rents its prisons to a management subsidiary run by the chairman's son. The subsidiary pays as much rent as possible, transforming its profits into tax-exempt "operating expenses" that it pays to the parent firm. The real estate trust, meanwhile, turns almost all of the rent money over to shareholders, thus sheltering its income from taxes as well. The scheme saves the trust $50 million a year in taxes—at the expense of CCA. On May 14, 1999 Prison Realty announced it would spend $86 million to prop up its troubled subsidiary. Its stock plummeted, and former shareholders filed a class-action lawsuit.

The real estate trust made out especially well in Youngstown. City officials eager to bring jobs to their depressed valley gave CCA 101 acres of land, free utility hookups and a five-year tax abatement for the prison. The company then sold the facility to the trust, pocketing $70 million. "This shows what private prisons are all about: profit," says Robert Hagan, a state senator from Youngstown. "That prison is nothing but a gulag."

Living Off Prisons

The CCA prison in Youngstown stands on a hillside once home to several thriving steel-related industries. The area is now home to four major new prisons and a host of jails. "Prisons have become Youngstown's new economic base," says labor historian and activist Staughton Lynd. "It's so pathetic to see this working-class town, which has quite a proud history of militant unionism, become one more rural backwater living off the presence of prisons."

Like other nonunion operations, private prisons make most of their money by hiring fewer people and paying them less. Former guards say two-thirds of the Youngstown officers never worked in corrections before, and starting wages were $1,300 a year less than those of their counterparts at state-run prisons. "They don't care about the corrections officers, and they don't care about the inmates," former guard Daniel Eshenbaugh told the *Cleveland Plain Dealer*. "Everything there is about money." Another former guard explained how CCA got workers to take food from inmates to boost profits. "They gave us a rundown saying two slices of bread per inmate costs this much," he said. "If you can cut corners here, it would mean a possible raise for us."

> "*[Private prison companies] don't care about the corrections officers, and they don't care about the inmates.*"

While Youngstown represents some of the worst abuses at CCA prisons, it is also the scene of the biggest victory for inmates since privatization began. On April 20, 1999 a federal judge in Akron approved a landmark settlement of the class-action lawsuit filed by prisoners. The company has agreed to make cash payments of up to $1,000 to every inmate and create a common fund to settle claims by those with serious injuries—for a total of $1.65 million, the second-highest award ever paid to inmates in a class-action lawsuit. Even more startling, the prisoners were joined in their suit by the City of Youngstown, which will now employ two independent monitors to oversee conditions and medical treatment at CCA. The monitors have the power to order the warden to fix inadequacies and to fine the company if it fails to act.

Accountability

"This is the first serious attempt to develop a way to hold a private prison accountable," attorney Al Gerhardstein said before the judge approved the settle-

125

ment. "The inmates and the city are working together to hold them to the level of staffing and medical care and programs they promised. That raises a question: If you refuse to wink and let them get away with abuses as long as they come in under budget, can they still make a profit?"

Some activists feel the settlement doesn't go far enough. "We need to shut private prisons down," says Lynd. "The care and rehabilitation of prisoners is not consistent with the profit motive."

But until profiteering from prisons is stopped, inmates welcome any step that reins in firms like CCA. "They run this place like GM or Ford," says James Neal, who urged the judge to approve the settlement. "It's like the defects in the Pinto. A $12 piece of steel would have corrected the problem, but their accountant showed it was cheaper not to fix it, even if people burned to death. That's the same way CCA runs prisons. If someone gets killed, so what? They just pay the family and give them some roses. They'll still be making millions off of misery."

Chapter 4

Should Prisons
Use Inmate Labor?

Prison Labor: An Overview

by Timothy Burn

About the author: *Timothy Burn is a journalist and a contributor to the* Washington Times.

Joseph Claggett's job is his life.

It keeps his mind occupied, puts a little money in his pocket. It provides a ray of hope for his otherwise bleak future.

But for a growing number of American companies, Claggett's job and thousands like it are robbing them of their most dependable customer: the federal government. And they want something done about it.

Claggett is a convicted drug dealer nearing the end of a lengthy prison sentence at the federal penitentiary here. He works about 40 hours a week as a production foreman guiding the assembly of wood office furniture bound for government offices around the nation. The buzz of saws and clack of hammers have occupied his once troubled mind for more years than he cares to admit.

"This work stops the confusion in men's minds. It gives us a chance to fend for ourselves and take care of our bills and personal needs," said Claggett, a burly man of 55 who has been in jail so long he can remember when cigarettes were free.

His $1.15 hourly wage pays for those little things, and more. When he is released in a few years he will have several thousand dollars to restart the life he left years ago in Southeast Washington.

"For so many of us, this job gives us something we can hold onto and call our own. It gives us work skills we can use to put back into the community when we get back into the free society," he said. But outside the prison walls a rising chorus of business owners are claiming the work he does is cutting into their bottom line and taking jobs away from law-abiding citizens.

"I understand that prisoners need some activities that provide skills training, but this antiquated policy that sets aside business for the prison system stacks the deck against honest, working men and women," said Henry Kroll, president of Western Government Supply, a San Francisco company that has lost more than a quarter of its business to prison workers.

In the past, those complaints have fallen on deaf ears of American policy-makers who believe that putting prisoners to work is a good idea.

But that could change in 1999. Congress is expected to consider two competing proposals to reform Claggett's employer, Federal Prison Industries (FPI), an agency created in 1934 to hire prison inmates to make products to be sold back to the government.

Reining In the Program

Under a federal mandate, FPI employs about one-sixth of the total federal prison population of 121,000, or 18,414 prisoners, to make a variety of products from furniture to clothing to missile containers.

While all federal prisoners are required to work by law, most are employed with menial tasks such as cleaning and laundry, earning just a few pennies an hour. FPI, also known as Unicor, aims to provide marketable skills training while instilling solid work habits.

The agency hires prisoners from a lengthy waiting list for manufacturing jobs that pay between 15 cents to $1.15 an hour. Half of all wages must pay for any outstanding fines, court fees or child support.

While critics tend to agree that keeping convicts busy and preparing them for freedom is a noble goal, they want lawmakers to rein in the program, which they say has become too large.

"[Prison labor] gives us work skills we can use to put back into the community when we get back into the free society."

Representative Peter Hoekstra, a Michigan Republican from a district that is home to several major furniture manufacturers, proposes compelling FPI to compete against private businesses for government contracts. Business leaders like Mr. Kroll think this will level the competition and improve FPI's operations.

Mr. Hoekstra's bill, first introduced in 1998, appeared headed for a mark-up session in the House Judiciary Committee until the committee became consumed with the impeachment of President Clinton.

Representative Bill McCollum, Florida Republican, has introduced a bill to gradually phase out mandatory sourcing and allow private companies to contract out production to prison workers. The bill is modeled after the Florida state prison work system, which is managed by a private company, Pride Enterprises Inc.

Both lawmakers plan to move aggressively on their proposals. An aide to Mr. McCollum said prison industry reform will be a top priority in 1999.

Work Force Booms

Until the 1990s the prison-worker agency fulfilled its mission in relative obscurity. But as the nation has become tougher on crime, the federal prison population has soared, from 24,000 inmates in 1980 to nearly 121,000 in 1999.

FPI has swelled along with the prison population, becoming the 37th largest supplier to the federal government.

Prison administrators in Washington see FPI as one way to manage the surging influx of new inmates, keeping them occupied and providing them work and life skills to make them better citizens once they leave.

> *"Business leaders . . . complain that it is unfair for the government to let a convict work force earn money making the same products that their civilian workers make."*

The rate of recidivism for FPI inmates is about 20 percent lower than for the rest of the prison population, according to recent studies.

By law, the federal government must set aside 25 percent of its contracts for FPI to provide such products as office furniture, clothing, metal frames, electronics, eye wear and printing. It also provides services for data conversion, repair, and labor and support.

But unions complain that the cheap labor is taking away jobs. Businesses lament the loss of valuable government contracts.

Business leaders, especially in the furniture industry, complain that it is unfair for the government to let a convict work force earn money making the same products that their civilian workers make.

For instance, Western Government Supply Incorporated, which supplies the federal government with ergonomic office furniture, says it has lost about 30 percent of its annual business to Unicor [an independent Federal Prison Industries Corporation].

The losses have been particularly hard since the furniture industry has been consolidating in the last decade and sending more production overseas.

"At our peak a decade ago we had about $2.2 million in sales, but now we are down to just $600,000 in 1998," Mr. Kroll said.

In August, the company lost one of its oldest clients, the Internal Revenue Service, to Unicor. It was a contract worth $125,000 and could have boosted the payroll for his marketing sales force that has shrunk from 18 to eight in the past three years. "I have to compete with Unicor for every product I sell, and it is just going to get worse as the prison system gets bigger," he said.

Businesses and labor unions have suggested that prison employees should work on tasks like recycling or disaster relief, areas in which private industry has little involvement. "We have been putting up with FPI for a long time, but now they are literally out of control," said Len Lorey, vice president of government affairs for Kimball International Inc. of Jasper, Indiana, which makes pianos and office furniture.

"Rather than having them continue to diversify and take more jobs away, we think the prisoner should be filling sand bags or helping with disaster relief using some sort of security detail."

FPI administrators have said there is not enough money to be made in those fields to keep the program self-sustaining, an argument that has stuck with lawmakers concerned about soaring prison costs.

More Attention

Steve Schwalb, president of FPI, said criticism of programs that help prisoners is nothing new. But the complaints have grown louder since 1998.

"The reason why we are getting more attention is because we are getting bigger, meaning we are generating more sales," he said. In 1997, FPI posted net sales of nearly $513 million from the more than 150 products it produces.

"The reason we are getting bigger is because there seems to be a pretty strong bipartisan public policy that says it's a good idea to put more people in prison for longer periods of time."

As more people are placed in the prison system, it gets more difficult for FPI to meet its goal of keeping 20 percent of the federal prison population working. That is why FPI is moving forward with plans to build 25 new plants inside prison walls to make more products and provide new services to the federal government.

Mr. Schwalb said he welcomes new proposals to improve the way the system works and minimize its impact on the private sector. But he said industry complaints about that impact are overblown since FPI's labor costs are considerably higher than in the private sector.

"Businesses and labor unions have suggested that prison employees should work on tasks like recycling or disaster relief, areas in which private industry has little involvement."

Most prisoners working for Unicor have never held down a full-time job and lack basic work skills. Mr. Schwalb said it takes at least four prison workers to complete the work of one person in the private sector.

The extra staff and guards needed to monitor the inmates more than offsets any advantage from producing products with lower-wage workers, he said.

Workers Wary

Claggett and his co-workers have heard the buzz over the future of Unicor. They fear the program will disappear like free soap and cigarettes did in the 1980s.

While the FPI workers build office furniture, the rest of the population is involved in menial tasks such as sweeping and laundry. Those jobs are barely supervised, and many of the inmates are able to stretch a small task into a day's work.

But for the 233 men working for FPI, the furniture making begins each morning at 7:30 a.m. sharp.

A staff of 14 administrators keeps track of the prison workers and monitors production levels. No armed guards watch over the plant.

The rules for conduct at Unicor are simple: If you start trouble, you're out, and the next guy on the list gets your job.

The waiting list to work for Unicor is based strictly on seniority. But inmates who have conduct problems never get to the top of the list. Claggett said such trouble almost never happens since most inmates are happy to be there.

He said many inmates in the general population, especially the newer ones, mock the FPI workers for toiling so hard and making so little money.

But, "I would not want to work no other place because it pays good and I'm always learning something new to go with what I got," he said.

"Most guys that have been in Unicor for a while feel the same way."

Claggett said more of the young inmates are starting to respect and admire the work ethic that has become such a force in his life.

"The younger guys just coming, in they pick that up and begin thinking the same way, and they begin to act like they want to work."

Prison Labor Is Beneficial

by Morgan Reynolds

About the author: *Morgan Reynolds is director of the Criminal Justice Center of the National Center for Policy Analysis, a nonprofit public policy think tank. He is also a professor of economics at Texas A&M University.*

The unemployment rate stands at 4.9 percent, the lowest since the Vietnam War. Employers looking for workers are finding that the supply of labor, even unskilled labor, is tight. As a result, Federal Reserve Board chief Alan Greenspan is worried about rising wages reigniting inflation.

However, more than a million Americans who could work—in fact, desperately need the skills that come only from real work—remain unproductive. These are our nation's prisoners. When idle prisoners are given the opportunity to engage in productive labor that pays a wage, they line up for it. Such work saves taxpayers' money and adds to the economy. Unfortunately, too many state and federal laws stand in the way.

The Growth in the Prison Population

The cost of operating the nation's prisons is soaring, along with the number of people in prisons.

- Since 1980 the state and federal prison population has increased from 316,000 to 1.2 million, and by the year 2002 the inmate population is expected to increase by another 400,000.
- Taxpayers are currently spending between $20,000 and $25,000 per year to house each of these criminals.
- The expense has reached about $30 billion, or $300 a year for every household in America.

Yet, despite a long-standing consensus in favor of gainful employment for convicts, idleness remains the norm behind bars. Perhaps half of all prisoners do some kind of work, counting housework (maintenance chores) and vocational training programs in the prisons. However, most of these jobs are part-time and produce no income for room and board, restitution and other ends.

In 1885 three-fourths of U.S. prison inmates were involved in productive la-

Reprinted, with permission, from "The Economic Impact of Prison Labor," by Morgan Reynolds, *NCPA Policy Brief Analysis*, no. 245, November 17, 1997.

bor, with the majority working under prison contract and leasing arrangements with private employers. However, as a result of the gradual adoption of federal and state regulations promoted by prisoner rights groups, organized labor and employers fearing competition, prison work declined dramatically. A 1994 survey of 46 correctional systems in the United States and seven in Canada found that only 9.4 percent of female and 7.75 percent of male inmates worked at jobs other than housekeeping and maintenance.

> *"Despite a long-standing consensus in favor of gainful employment for convicts, idleness remains the norm behind bars."*

Skeptics of welfare reform argued that only a small percentage of welfare recipients could be gainfully employed. But once states got the welfare-to-work incentives right, welfare recipients went to work in droves, cutting welfare caseloads by 60 percent in some states and up to 80 percent in some Wisconsin counties. Prison work can achieve similar successes.

In a survey by the Prison Enterprise Institute, prison industry managers frequently mentioned 25 percent of prisoners as a desired target for employment. But putting a majority of prisoners—who are generally young, healthy and able-bodied—to work is a reachable goal.

Since prisoners have relatively little else to do, what could we reasonably expect under an aggressive expansion of private production by prisoners?

- A full-time job means about 2,000 hours of work per year (40 hours per week times 50 weeks).
- At an average wage of $7.00 an hour, inmates could average $14,000 in gross earnings per year.

The Impact of Prison Labor on Taxpayers

One of the most promising proposals to reduce the cost of criminal justice is to increase the amount of productive work performed by prisoners. Eighty percent of the income earned by prisoners who work is customarily used to reduce the financial burden on taxpayers and for victim compensation. Thus about $11,000 per prison worker would be available. The remainder could help prisoners' families, pay personal expenses and be set aside as savings for use after release.

By 2002, the prison population is projected to increase to 1.6 million. If half of the prisoners could be employed by private enterprise during that time, their work would reduce taxpayer costs by almost $9 billion per year, or about 25 percent of the total cost of prison support.

One of the most important benefits of prisoner work is that it reduces the recidivism rate. A federal Post-Release Employment Project (PREP) study confirms that employed prisoners do better than those who do not work.

After release to halfway houses, participants in the PREP study were 24 percent more likely to get a full-time or day labor job than those who had not worked in prison. Those who had worked in prison also earned more than those who had not and were more likely to move on to a better-paying job. Only 6.6 percent of those who worked in prison had their parole revoked or were charged with committing a new crime during their first year of supervised release. This compares to 10.1 percent of the group who had not worked in prison.

These findings hold up over a much longer period. Most participants in a follow-up to the PREP study had been released for at least eight years and some for as long as 12 years. Prison work and training programs seem to have been especially effective in reducing the likelihood of recidivism in the long term.

The Impact of Prison Labor on the Economy

Besides the indirect benefits of reducing the cost to taxpayers of housing prisoners and reducing the recidivism rate, prisoner work has two direct economic benefits. First, prison industries must purchase materials from businesses outside the prison, thus creating a demand for the services of other workers. For example:

- Prisoners involved in information services such as travel reservations, telemarketing and data entry need computers for their jobs.
- Those involved in manufacturing require sheet metal, cloth and other raw materials.
- Others involved in assembly jobs rely on manufactured goods such as electronic circuit boards, cables and cable harnesses.

Second, prisoners have the potential to produce valuable goods and services consumers want to buy. Prison industries produced more than $1 billion worth of goods and services in 1994, mostly for other government agencies. However, since prison industry is usually state run rather than privately run, the output is often shoddy, overpriced merchandise that other state agencies must buy from the prison industry monopoly. The largest prison supplier was the Federal Bureau of Prisons with $433 million in output for federal agencies, yet the system employed only 16,000 inmates out of 61,000 inmates eligible to work (i.e., those not in solitary confinement, considered dangerous or being transferred) from its total of 85,000 inmates.

> *"If half of the prisoners could be employed by private enterprise . . . their work would reduce taxpayer costs by almost $9 billion per year."*

Though any type of productive prison work is good, private enterprise would make it even better, and given more latitude in creating prison industry it could achieve dramatic results. For example, in 1923, when the private sector still played a significant role in prisoner employment, productivity was four times greater under private than under public control, even when the same industries were compared.

Consider a prisoner who is earning $14,000 per year. His productivity adds to the economy just as does that of a noninstitutionalized person. If 800,000 prisoners worked—a labor force equal to those of Wyoming, Alaska and Vermont combined—their productivity would add more than $20 billion to the economy.

Wouldn't Prison Labor Steal Private-Sector Jobs?

Quite the contrary. Once at work, the prisoner is a job creator, on balance, because prison production requires new purchases from free-world businesses. That means jobs and higher real wages in the rest of the economy.

Everyone recognizes that getting able-bodied adults off welfare and into productive jobs is a social boon, and we have been willing to subsidize that transition from welfare to work. The same thing should be true for prison labor.

While some are concerned that wages in prison would be below market wages, thereby robbing jobs from regular workers, in a competitive marketplace wages reflect productivity. Prison wages are typically lower because prison labor is less productive.

Prison work has many opponents, as did proposals to put welfare recipients to work—and for many of the same reasons. But states that have aggressively moved to "workfare" have shown that the vast majority of welfare recipients can become productive, benefit the economy and build new lives. We should expect no less from the nation's prisoners.

Prison Labor Is Essential to Rehabilitation

by *Christianity Today*

About the author: Christianity Today *is a magazine devoted to issues pertaining to the evangelical Christian community.*

For one key period of his life, Ron Humphrey worked a typical eight-hour day as a computer-systems manager, followed by another four hours after dinner. He worked Saturdays as well.

Humphrey was not working for a cruel, Dickensian boss. As an inmate in a federal prison, Humphrey found his work to be a constructive escape from the ennui of his cell.

Unfortunately, few prison inmates have the opportunity for gainful employment. The federal prison population in the United States has nearly doubled since 1990, and the total U.S. prison population is now almost 1.2 million. Our rate of incarceration is second only to that of Russia. Remarkably, the percentage of prisoners working has dropped dramatically: from about 75 percent in 1885 to about 8 percent in 1995. When modern "penitentiaries" were founded in the 1790s, they were designed on Christian principles, with work as a key force in helping prisoners toward reform. But public concern grew over competition for jobs from the prison labor force, especially with the coming of the Great Depression, during which 33 states passed laws prohibiting the sale of convict-made goods on the open market. Federal laws passed since then prompted an assistant attorney general in Arizona to say, "The original conception of the penitentiary was . . . turned on its head. Prison labor, once viewed as indispensable for restoring a healthy relationship between the criminal and society, was made literally a federal offense."

The sheer volume of prison idleness demands a massive attitudinal shift on the part of society, so that private enterprise will link with public administration for the betterment of offenders and society. The benefits of prison employment (not to be confused with the economic exploitation of offenders) are evident:

Reprinted, with permission, from "Let the Prisoners Work," editorial, *Christianity Today*, February 9, 1998.

enhanced mental health for the prisoners, reduced violence, beefed-up family support, preserved marriages, diminished violence and recidivism, and increased restitution paid to victims of crimes.

Beating the Odds

Humphrey himself is a testimony to these benefits. He has been out of prison nearly a decade and is now circulation manager for the Prison Fellowship publication *Inside Journal*. Prison work is a mental-health issue, he says. "You keep yourself busy or you go nuts," he told *Christianity Today*. "You have to look for ways to get through it without your mind being destroyed."

Marilyn Moses of the National Institute of Justice agrees. "From an offender perspective," says Moses, "doing nothing but 'three hots [hot meals] and a cot' is terrible." Indeed, says a Justice Fellowship report, work "can prevent some of the frustration that comes from idleness," frustration that often results in fights and violent assaults. When 85 percent of Minnesota's prison population was working, a Justice Fellowship report points out, it had one of the lowest rates of prison violence in the country.

> *"Prisoners who work are not just killing time: they are doing something constructive."*

But prisoners who work are not just killing time: they are doing something constructive. In Humphrey's case, work was a way of participating in the life of his family. His six-day work week allowed him to pay the rent for his wife and four children, while she could use income from her nursing-home jobs on medical bills and food. But more significantly, "My monthly check indicated to us that I was still a participating member of the family."

This helped the Humphreys beat the odds: 85 percent of men who go into prison married are divorced by the time they are released. Of the remaining 15 percent, half see their marriages fail within their first year back in society. Humphrey believes his contribution to his family's maintenance created the context of confidence and caring in which his marriage could survive.

Clearly, the social cost of allowing prisoners' families to fall into a pattern of social dependency is enormous, while the payback for investing in prison industries is measured not only in the economic value of goods produced and incarceration subsidies, but also in the incalculable value of families preserved.

Prisoners Who Pay

Prison labor also allows for offenders (where appropriate) to make some degree of restitution to their victims. Restitution teaches them that their victims are human like themselves by forging a personal and financial connection between victim and victimizer. Unfortunately, our courts too rarely consider the possibility of prisoners participating in restitution. In 1986, according to a Department of Justice study, 36 percent of felons placed on probation (including

52 percent of burglars) were ordered to pay restitution. But only 14 percent of felons sent to prison were ordered to pay restitution. The courts must realize more fully the potential for inmates to pay, literally, for their crimes.

Recidivism Rates

The maturity that comes from participating in meaningful prison work—not the same as slave labor or chain gangs—shows in recidivism rates. In one study, after release to halfway houses, only 6.6 percent of participants who had worked in prison had their parole revoked or were charged with committing a new crime in their first year of supervised release, compared to 10.1 percent of those who had not worked in prison. Another study found that after three years the recidivism rate of those who had worked for Wisconsin's state prison industries program was 15 percent lower than it was for those who had not.

Given such a positive record for prison industries, who could oppose them? In a strong economy, hardly anybody. Still, prison industries have a long way to go to achieve the effectiveness and public acceptance they should have even though Congress in 1979 relaxed the restrictions against prison industries. In October 1997, for example, certain manufacturing interests rallied around a bill introduced in Congress that would end the requirement that federal agencies should shop first with federal government-run inmate work programs. Perhaps that cozy marketing arrangement with federal agencies should be annulled. But October's protests were framed in terms of prisoners "taking job opportunities away from thousands of honest, hard-working Americans." That's political rhetoric, not reality. Case studies show that when private industry contracts for prison work, American jobs are saved, as low-skill, low-wage tasks are retained in our prisons instead of being shipped outside the country.

> *"I can either lie on my prison bunk and cost the taxpayers about $16,000 a year, or I can be out here . . . paying back society."*

We all have choices. As one inmate told Charles Colson, "I can either lie on my prison bunk and cost the taxpayers about $16,000 a year, or I can be out here doing something productive, paying back society." Or as former Chief Justice Burger framed the question: "Do we want prisoners to return to society as predators or as producers?"

Prison Laborers Learn Marketable Skills

by Michael N. Harrell

About the author: *Michael N. Harrell is an employee of Prison Rehabilitative Industries and Diversified Enterprises (PRIDE), a private, nonprofit corporation that manages correctional industries inside Florida's state prison system. The following viewpoint is adapted from his testimony before the House Subcommittee on Crime on October 30, 1997.*

Prison Rehabilitative Industries and Diversified Enterprises, Inc. (PRIDE), headquartered in St. Petersburg, Florida, is a private non-profit corporation authorized to manage and operate the state's correctional industries inside Florida's state prisons. PRIDE operates 57 industries in 22 correctional institutions with revenues in 1996 of $85 million. A cross-section of leaders in business, education and government are members of the corporation's Board of Directors. Appointed by the Executive Office of the Governor, they provide leadership and oversight.

Provides Accredited Inmate Training

Prison inmates learn marketable job skills when they train and work in the PRIDE industries that manufacture 3,000 different products and services. Business professionals train the inmates within a private enterprise environment that demands a strong work ethic and a focus on quality customer service—the soft skills demanded by today's employers. The corporation's commitment to provide acknowledged industrial job training resulted in 85% of PRIDE's training businesses and operations being independently certified by accredited institutions; e.g., the Florida Department of Education, Florida A&M University, and the University of Florida as well as business and trade associations and organizations such as the National Institute of Automotive Service Excellence.

When fully-trained PRIDE inmate workers leave prison, they carry with them credentials of achievement in job skills that meet the requirements of today's businesses. PRIDE also provides comprehensive post-release support for

Reprinted from Michael N. Harrell's testimony before the U.S. House Committee on the Judiciary, Subcommittee on Crime and Criminal Justice, October 30, 1997.

PRIDE ex-workers that includes job placement, housing, transportation and other services that are critical to an ex-offender's successful transition into society. Over the past five years, an annual average of 88 percent of PRIDE ex-workers remain out of prison.

As a quality-driven industrial manufacturing business, PRIDE Enterprises relies on the sales of its products and services to continue and expand the prison industries and operations that will offer more relevant job training to more inmates. Since 1985 no public funds have been provided to support the industry operations—in fact, PRIDE returns dollars to the state each year.

> *"When fully-trained . . . inmate workers leave prison, they carry with them credentials of achievement in job skills that meet the requirements of today's businesses."*

PRIDE also absorbs the high costs of inmate on-the-job training created by an annual average of 100% turnover rate of inmate workers, large amounts of scrapped materials and an average six hour work day. However, because of its experience in working within a constant training mode, the corporation can through good sound business principles, strategies and quality measurements operate successfully. PRIDE workers produce quality products and services that are internationally competitive. A good example is the recent achievements of PRIDE's Cross City print industry. For seven consecutive years, this print industry has entered and won top awards in the International Screen Printers Association contest. It is the only prison industry competing with over 200 major companies from 32 countries. Just last week, this "world class quality" industry again won two golds, one silver and two honorable mentions, bringing the total to six golds, five silvers, two bronzes, and five honorable mentions achieved over the past seven years.

Tax Savings

Additionally, PRIDE lessens the tax burden of Florida citizens by making voluntary payments directly to the state that average approximately $1 million per year. These funds are deposited into the state's Correctional Work Programs Trust Fund to be used systemwide by the Department of Corrections for training and educating other inmates, most of whom are not participants in PRIDE industries. PRIDE also contributes another $1 million annually to the state for victim restitution and for the provision of inmate support services that includes the critical post-release transition support (job placement, housing, continuing education, tools and transportation to job interviews).

Business professionals who train the inmates make up the majority of PRIDE's 400 employees. Again, like any other private sector corporation, PRIDE provides a competitive salary and benefit package to its employees, who are not civil servants. Again, the costs are absorbed by the generation of revenues received from the sale of goods and services manufactured by PRIDE.

Although PRIDE is a private corporation, as a non-profit company it does not have shareholders and it does not issue stock. Any and all profits the company achieves are put back into the company to expand new businesses, to modernize existing industries or to provide the State of Florida contributions for reducing the costs of incarceration and the enhancement of state property. Since PRIDE's industrial factories and agricultural industries are located on state property, all physical improvements increase the value of the state's assets. . . .

Another critical component to the successful operation of PRIDE Enterprises is public-private partnerships. Businesses throughout the state, as well as national and state trade associations and organizations, serve an important role by providing assistance to PRIDE that includes business planning, the previously mentioned review of inmate job training processes, and the actual hiring of PRIDE ex-offenders. Over three hundred of these businesses have been commended by Governor Lawton Chiles for their valuable contributions. Organized labor in Florida has been a partner with PRIDE. . . .

At the same time, the corporation is looking for other ways to help Florida [strengthen] its economy. One avenue is to ask businesses to consider workers in the prison industries first as an alternative resource option before looking to move their business offshore. Reeves Southeastern, a nationally and internationally recognized leader in fencing, perimeter building materials and high security products, entered into a partnership with PRIDE

"[Prison labor] is a win-win for the inmates because they will be trained in marketable job skills that translate well into today's job market."

under the federally authorized Prison Industries Enhancement (PIE) program. The partnership expanded production capacity for Reeves Southeastern and job skill training opportunities for PRIDE inmate workers. PRIDE workers assemble metal components for inclusion into Reeves Southeastern's product lines such as galvanized steel tubing used for frames for portable, customer-installed dog kennels and fence gates. Given the excellent quality of products and services PRIDE produced for Reeves Southeastern, Reeves Southeastern has decided to expand its business partnership with PRIDE. Recently, Reeves hired one of PRIDE's former workers when he was released from prison—another great benefit to the inmate worker and to the company, which is getting a willing and skilled worker. . . .

Private employers who partner with PRIDE find new labor options, allowing them to redeploy their civilian workforce more effectively, and companies surrounding that prison venture feel the economic ripple effects, too. Florida's economic future depends on its citizens being productive, including those in prison and those rebuilding their lives free of welfare assistance. Many ex-felons and their families are part of the welfare spectrum. Businesses typically cite lack of available skilled labor as a reason for sending work overseas or not being able to expand their operations. By strengthening partnerships with prison work programs that produce quality products and services demanded in today's market, businesses can also strengthen Florida's potential for retention, growth and recruitment for new companies.

Prison Industries Are a Productive Component of Society

In summary, PRIDE wants to continue to replicate the effectiveness of the recommitment rate of inmates released from the company's industries. To expand this effectiveness, PRIDE is aggressively pursuing partnerships with the private sector. This is a win-win for the inmates because they will be trained in marketable job skills that translate well into today's job market and enable them to become productive citizens instead of turning to crime again and preying on more victims. It's a win-win for the state's citizens in terms of public safety. It's a win-win for the business community because they can expand their operations in an increasing tight labor market. It's a win-win for the State of Florida because economic development occurs. It's a win-win for the nation's economy because prison industries encourage manufacturers to keep jobs from going offshore.

Inmate Chain Gangs Are an Effective Deterrent to Crime

by Charlie Crist

About the author: *Charlie Crist, a Republican, is a Florida state senator.*

The official nickname of Florida is "The Sunshine State." The state has the environment of paradise. With gorgeous waters, sandy beaches and the cultural splendor of its major cities, Florida has a lot to offer both citizens and tourists alike.

But for the past few years, a more appropriate nickname for Florida would be "The Crime State." Criminals have murdered, raped, robbed and maimed innocent citizens. The statistics reveal a grim reality. In December 1994, the Federal Bureau of Investigation rated Florida number one in violent crime. In May 1995, the FBI reported that the three most violent cities in the nation were Florida's—Ft. Lauderdale, Tampa and Miami. And in November of 1995, the FBI released new and equally disturbing statistics which showed that Florida has three of the top five most violent cities in the nation—Miami, Gainesville and Tallahassee. According to the Florida Department of Law Enforcement, every three minutes and 39 seconds another violent crime is committed in Florida.

As a state senator, it didn't take this kind of flood of frightening statistics for me to realize there was a problem. Constituents told me. They watch the news, as I do, and see the statistics played out over and over again. They tell me they are afraid to leave their homes at night.

In late 1994, when I was appointed chairman of the Ways and Means Subcommittee on Criminal Justice, which funds criminal justice programs in Florida, I decided to tour some prisons to see how money is spent on criminal justice. What I found was appalling.

Florida's prisons have basketball courts, sand volleyball pits, racquetball courts and baseball diamonds. Inmates enjoy weightlifting, arts and crafts, and amenities such as boccie balls for Italian-style bowling. The Florida Department of Corrections informed me that less than half of all inmates work, and

Reprinted with the permission of the American Correctional Association, Lanham, Maryland, from "Chain Gangs Are Right for Florida," by Charlie Crist, *Corrections Today*, April 1996.

many work for only about four hours a day. It was abundantly clear to me that inmates had too much freedom in prison.

Correctional officers told me that these amenities were necessary to keep inmates busy, so as to minimize the security risk that is caused by idle time. Yet, they also confessed to me that they would rather see inmates work.

It occurred to me, after touring a number of prison facilities, that Florida was sending the wrong message to criminals. In effect, we were telling criminals that if they commit a crime, they go to a place not unlike summer camp.

After seeing prisons and talking with state correctional officers and other officers who were interested in a better system of criminal justice, the answer seemed obvious: We needed to replace play with work.

Certainly inmates can work within the confines of the prison, and I believe they should. The prison system I envision is self-sustaining, where inmates grow their own food, do their own carpentry and plumbing, and handle the upkeep of the prison.

But I believe that convicted criminals should also work on our highways and byways, in visible places where would-be criminals can see the price of committing crime. Presently, nonviolent criminals do engage in this kind of work, but for obvious safety reasons, violent criminals cannot. That's inequitable. Chains provide additional security that, along with armed guards, keep our citizens and tourists safe while giving criminals the opportunity to work.

> *"[Chain gangs] are a visible form of punishment that sends the message that if you commit a crime, you will be punished, and it will not be pleasant."*

Chain gangs offer a number of benefits, particularly when they replace the kind of broken system we had in Florida. First, work on the chain gang is an appropriate punishment. It puts criminals to work. It gives them the opportunity to give back to the society they have taken from. Chain gangs and hard work ensure that prison is not pleasant, which is what society wants and criminals need.

Additionally, chain gangs are a useful prison management tool. Inmates work all day, so they are tired at the end of the day. This eliminates the need for recreation as a management tool during the day. I also support providing education to inmates at night.

Perhaps most important in the long run, chain gangs serve as a deterrent. They are a visible form of punishment that sends the message that if you commit a crime, you will be punished, and it will not be pleasant.

All this adds up to justice. Ultimately, it all adds up to freedom for law-abiding citizens. It means that we can get back the Florida where our children can play without fear, where our senior citizens can take evening strolls, where all of us can enjoy the environment, the beaches and the cultural splendor that make Florida the paradise that "The Sunshine State" should be.

Prison Labor Is Not Beneficial

by Jane Slaughter

About the author: *Jane Slaughter is a Detroit-based labor writer.*

Start talking about "prison labor," and people tend to fall into two categories. One is appalled at the exploitation implied: workers locked up, overseen by guards, with no say in their wages, conditions, or anything else. But the other group sees a chance to "make prisons pay" and to get tough on crime. Back in the 1970s, Chief Justice Warren Burger called for turning prisons into "factories with fences." Today, Burger's words are coming true, with consequences that may be as serious for workers on the outside as for those who labor behind bars.

The Growing Number of Inmate Laborers

The number of prisoners who work for private, profit-making companies or state-controlled industries—around 80,000—is still relatively small compared to the skyrocketing prison population.

But the numbers are growing fast, urged along by advocates in government and by companies who see prison labor as a closer-to-home alternative to production in Asia and Mexico.

"It's about time we stopped being ashamed of our resources and began putting them to work," says Representative Stephen Matthew, chair of a Congressional committee studying prison labor. Matthew says his goal is to have half of all prisoners holding down inside jobs by the year 2000.

Consider these trends:

- a phenomenal increase in the number of people behind bars—1.9 million today, driving towards one percent of the total population—propelled by the lock 'em up mentality prevalent in legislatures;
- fewer and fewer good jobs available, as the supposedly "booming" economy creates mostly low-wage or temporary or part-time jobs (or all three);
- welfare recipients forced into low-paid jobs in competition with other working-class people, under the heading of "welfare reform."

Reprinted, with permission, from "Captive Labor: Jobs Without Justice," by Jane Slaughter, *The Witness*, November 1998.

Then recall the rhetoric that conservatives use to describe members of what they call "the underclass"—"welfare queens" sucking up the tax dollars of hard-working citizens, criminals watching TV in jail, likewise on the tax dollars of those same law-abiding citizens. Given all this, it's not hard to believe that policy makers have in mind a two-pronged "solution" to the perceived problem of the underclass: low-paid, poverty-sustaining jobs for the women, even lower-paid jobs in jail for the men. As one advocate mused in an Internet posting, "[Prison] labor is the carpet under which can be swept those who fall out the bottom of the system, and it's a profit center as well! . . . It seems to be the only government-sponsored program that 'deals with' inner-city unemployment."

> *"It was today's prison-building binge that . . . sent lawmakers looking for ways to make money from convicts' work."*

Slave Labor?

In a collection of essays by prisoners, *The Celling of America,* prisoner Paul Wright, co-editor of *Prison Legal News,* notes that Americans mistakenly believe that slavery was ended by the Thirteenth Amendment. In truth, Wright points out, "slavery and involuntary servitude" were abolished, in the words of the Constitution, "except as punishment for crimes whereof the party shall have been duly convicted." After the Civil War, it was common for newly freed slaves to be "duly convicted," sent to jail, and then leased out to private employers.

In the 1930s, spurred by Depression unemployment, Congress forbade the interstate transport of prison-made goods made for less than minimum wage, effectively shutting down the private use of prison labor. It was today's prison-building binge that once again sent lawmakers looking for ways to make money from convicts' work. In 1979, Congress created a program to help bring private companies into prisons. From 1980 to 1994, sales by prison industries, private and state-run, rose from $392 million to $1.31 billion, as the number of federal and state prisoners working in prison industries jumped by 358 percent. Some industry officials estimate that by 2000 prison industries' sales will hit $8.9 billion.

Required to Work

Some prisoner activists, such as Paul Wright, call prison work "slave labor," arguing that it is not truly voluntary. According to the American Federation of Labor and Congress of Industrial Organizations (AFL-CIO), 21 states have passed laws requiring prisoners to work, and federal prisoners are required to work as well. Just as important, taking a job can reduce your sentence, often on a day worked per day served basis, and not taking one can subject you to penalties that lengthen your sentence.

Even at the pitifully low wages paid, prisoners take jobs for the money. Alice Lynd, co-founder of a prisoners' advocacy group called Prison Forum in

Youngstown, Ohio, explains, "I have a friend who gets $17 a month for tutoring. People working for Ohio Penal Industries get as much as $45 a month. It creates a class system within the prison as to who's got money for the commissary and who hasn't." One prisoner doing data entry at San Quentin said, "The food here sucks and a can of tuna fish costs 95 cents in the commissary, so I am really glad to have this job."

Prison Pay

Courts have ruled that the Fair Labor Standards Act, which mandates the minimum wage for free labor, does not apply to government-employed prisoners. Federal UNICOR [an independent federal prison industries corporation] inmates are paid between 23 cents and $1.15 per hour, and up to 50 percent of that may be deducted. Private companies in prison are required to pay the minimum wage. Whatever the nominal wage, however, prisoners see only a small portion of it. Prison officials make deductions for room and board, taxes, family support, victim restitution, and savings for release. A Unibase employee at Lebanon Correctional Institution in Ohio, for example, makes 47 cents an hour for data entry, and a sewing machine operator at Soledad in California makes 45 cents.

> *"Not taking [a prison job] can subject you to penalties that lengthen your sentence."*

If prisoners have incentives to take prison jobs, private companies have equally strong motivation to locate behind bars. A publication from the Department of Justice spells it out: "Inmates represent a readily available and dependable source of entry-level labor that is a cost-effective alternative to work forces found in Mexico, the Caribbean Basin, Southeast Asia, and the Pacific Rim countries."

Company executives delight that prisoner-workers never get stuck in traffic (though they are subject to periodic prison-wide lockdowns). Nor do they receive benefits or vacations. And they fit well with companies' focus on "flexibility"—available when needed for surges in demand, returned to their cells, with no unemployment pay, when the market sags. Prisoners can be fired for any or no reason, including back-talk, and they are not allowed to unionize, much less to strike.

On top of these incentives, the government often provides handsome subsidies to entrepreneurs, such as leasing them space at very low rates or subsidies to buy equipment. An ad from the Wisconsin Department of Corrections asks business owners, "Can't Find Workers? A Willing Workforce Waits."

Perhaps the most bizarre rationale for prison labor is that it keeps jobs in the U.S. "We can put a Made-in-the-U.S.A. label on our product," one executive told a Justice Department researcher. Companies argue that prison jobs would otherwise be done by workers in Sri Lanka or El Salvador. The president of multinational Unibase, with workers inside three Ohio prisons, says that keeping work in the state is part of his "sales pitch."

It's easy to imagine a scenario in which a worker loses his job, commits a crime out of desperation, and then ends up working for his former company in jail. But at least he's got the job, not the foreign competition!

Rehabilitation?

Occasionally an advocate of prison labor will claim it's good for prisoners (as opposed to state or private coffers). The idea is that prison jobs teach work habits to those who've seldom held a steady job. One study, for example, showed that inmates employed by Badger State Industries in Wisconsin had a 15 percent lower recidivism rate than other inmates.

But others doubt that prison work will help prisoners once they return to society. For one thing, prison employers tend to cherry-pick the "best" prisoners, those with work histories and good records. Many managers set up the hiring scene as much as possible like private-sector ventures, with applications and interviews. So those hired are those most likely to make it on the outside in any case.

Second, most prison jobs are specifically designed not to require marketable skills. The Justice Department passes along the advice of a manager at a South Carolina firm: "Keep it simple—put the least complex sewing jobs you have inside the prison." Alice Lynd points out, "Sewing blue jeans isn't done outside prisons, it's done overseas. When they get out they won't be able to run down to a plant and get a job."

Third, although punching a behind-bars time clock is said to teach a "work ethic," the stultifying nature of the low-skill job could also carry the lesson that work is something to be avoided at all costs.

Competition

With the American workforce already battered by downsizing, privatization, contracting out, and the dislocation of jobs to overseas factories, workers' organizations are becoming alarmed by the rapid growth of prison work. "Prison labor," says the AFL-CIO, "is being used today to perform work in both the private and public sectors ordinarily done by free workers."

Under the 1979 Prison Industries Enhancement law, private companies who want to operate in jail must pay the "prevailing wage." They must consult with and win approval from union leaders in the area; their industry must be one with no local unemployment; and the local labor market should not be affected.

> *"It's easy to imagine a scenario in which a worker loses his job, commits a crime out of desperation, and then ends up working for his former company in jail."*

But as the examples below show, these rules are apparently ignored:

- In Arizona, a hog slaughtering plant closed down, costing union workers their jobs. The plant then reopened as a joint venture between the Department of Corrections and the state's Pork Producers Association.
- In Wisconsin, Fabry Glove & Mitten cut wages and slashed outside jobs by 40 percent after hiring inmates at the Green Bay Correctional Institution.
- In Utah, asbestos removal companies say that prison labor has virtually driven them out of business. "We find it ironic that they are putting an industry out of business that they are purportedly training people to work in," said a spokesperson.
- Companies in the government-supply business say that UNICOR's rapid expansion has cost 2,000 jobs in furniture-making since the late 1980s.
- A private prison run by Wackenhut in Lockhart, Texas, houses a company called LTI which assembles circuit boards for IBM and Texas Instruments. Wackenhut built LTI a brand-new facility

> *"Most prison jobs are specifically designed not to require marketable skills."*

(using prisoner labor) and charges the company a rent of $1 per year. To top it off, LTI gets a tax abatement from the city.

But before this cozy arrangement, LTI operated a circuit board plant in nearby Austin, employing 150 workers. The company laid them all off and moved its equipment to Lockhart.
- DPAS, a literature assembly firm, closed its facility in Tecate, Mexico, in favor of San Quentin.

Prevention, Not Bogus Cures

Youngstown, Ohio, where Alice Lynd lives and works, was devastated by the steel mill closings of the 1980s. She helped found the Prison Forum group after Youngstown officials hailed the construction of a new "Supermax" prison there as a job-creation coup. Prison Forum has drawn up a platform on prison labor that would protect both imprisoned workers and those outside the walls. Besides banning the displacement of outside jobs, it would give prison workers the right to unionize and strike, or, at the very least, to report their grievances to an outside labor organization to advocate on their behalf.

Lynd is a Quaker whose long-time activism has ranged from union support to draft counseling during the Vietnam war. Her work with prisoners, she believes, is "consistent with traditional Quaker concerns; it has roots that go way back." Prison Forum includes a retired schoolteacher, professors of criminal justice and English literature, two steelworkers and the religious education director of a Unitarian church.

As an attorney, Lynd is able to work directly with prisoners while also taking education into the community. "People tend to think of criminals as people who are like barbarians," she says, "people who are outside the society. But most of them are going to return to society, and they may have a more difficult time than they had before to reestablish themselves in a constructive mode, rather than go from bad to worse." She wants to "assist by giving people hope, help them figure out how their future can amount to anything, how they will make it on the outside."

Unfortunately, she doesn't see prison jobs, in their current form, as a big part of the solution. "Some major plants will hire ex-convicts," she says, "but there are an awful lot of occupations where they're not going to.

"We need to do much more at the prevention end. Increasingly repressive prisons and longer terms are not meeting society's needs. Jobs, education, assistance to get off drugs are being shortchanged to try to deal with it at the wrong end of the problem."

Prison Labor Threatens the Jobs of Law-Abiding Citizens

by Ann Hoffman

About the author: *Ann Hoffman is the legislative director for the Union of Needletrade, Industrial and Textile Employees (UNITE). The following viewpoint is adapted from her testimony before the House Subcommittee on Crime, June 25, 1998.*

The general public overwhelmingly favors protecting the jobs of hardworking Americans from the unjust competition created by proposals such as H.R. 4100, which is known as the Prison Industries Reform Act of 1998. On May 5, 1998, the Enterprise Prison Institute released a public opinion survey related to inmate work. The survey asked respondents whether they agreed or disagreed with the following statement: "The only way I would support any company setting up in prison is if there were absolute assurances we were not just shifting jobs from the community into prison."

By more than a two to one margin, respondents agreed or strongly agreed with this statement. However, even though Americans want "absolute assurances" that prison labor will not have adverse effects on jobs in their communities, the proposed legislation discards all previous attempts to curb unjust competition, and extends prison labor initiatives to unprecedented levels. This legislation would lead to even more law-abiding Americans losing their jobs to those members of our society that have been incarcerated.

Lost Jobs

Even under the current status of prison labor programs in many states, thousands of law-abiding Americans have lost jobs to the unfair competition from incarcerated workers. For example, prisoners in Washington state shrink-wrapped the software that had been packaged by Microsoft employees. South

Reprinted from Ann Hoffman's testimony before the U.S. House Committee on the Judiciary, Subcommittee on Crime and Criminal Justice, June 25, 1998.

Carolina prisoners made the Victoria's Secret lingerie that was once made by workers in the private sector. Some TWA reservation officers have lost their jobs to convicts in a California prison.

The proposed legislation repeals the existing prohibition on the sale of inmate-produced products in interstate commerce, and thus makes it even easier for states to create prison industries that compete with non-prison labor. Thousands of law-abiding workers have already lost jobs with the current level of prison labor initiatives. Many thousands more will lose jobs if prison labor initiatives are allowed to expand.

> *"Thousands of law-abiding Americans have lost jobs to the unfair competition from incarcerated workers."*

H.R. 4100 would also expand Federal Prison Industries (FPI) by extending its mandatory-source rule to include all forms of services as well as products. Under current law, federal agencies are required to buy products offered by FPI, even if they could procure the same or better products at lower cost, and faster from commercial companies. The proposed expansion of the mandatory-source rule to services would simply force government agencies to make even more inefficient purchases at the taxpayer's expense.

Moreover, the mandatory-source rule would create new safety and security risks. For example, if convicts were given personal information, such as credit card numbers, income figures, addresses and phone numbers as part of information-processing jobs, both government employees and private citizens would be exposed to abuse. Furthermore, if convicts were placed in federal buildings to perform janitorial services or in national parks to perform landscaping, federal employees and vacationing families would be put at risk.

Unfair Competition

This bill would also expand Federal Prison Industries by authorizing the unrestricted sale of FPI products in the commercial marketplace, as long as they are "foreign-made goods" or "assembled goods." The combined effect of all of these exceptions is that virtually every product for the commercial market will be eligible for federal prison production, and even more law-abiding workers in virtually every industry would be at risk of unfair competition from prison labor.

According to the bill, a product will be considered a "foreign-made good" if the Bureau of Labor Statistics determines that 95% or more of the dollar amount sold in the United Sates is fabricated "in a foreign place." However, just because an item was made in a foreign country one year does not mean it would not be made in a non-prison setting in the United States the next year. In fact, many corporations manufacture a given product in this country in one year and elsewhere the next, or make a blue shirt in the United States and the identical shirt in a different color in another country at the same time. The Union of

Needletrade, Industrial and Textile Employees' (UNITE) experience with FPI manipulation of market data in the recent case of glove industry expansion leads us to anticipate similar manipulation in defining "foreign-made goods." Moreover, this provision will encourage other countries to replace U.S. made exports with their own prison-made products, thereby further endangering American jobs.

The use of the term "assembled good" makes it possible that virtually any product produced for the commercial market may be deemed as an acceptable FPI industry. However, if by some chance, a particular FPI product did not qualify under one of the two provisions, the product would only need to be designated as a "Private Sector Project" or "Prison Industries Enhancement Project" in order to gain access to the commercial market.

Gainful Employment?

H.R. 4100 even seems to undercut the rehabilitative benefits of inmate work opportunities by repealing the provision of FPI's authorizing statute that calls for "maximum opportunity to acquire a knowledge and skill in trades and occupations which will provide them with a means of earning a livelihood upon release." To the extent that employment programs would still be designed to train prisoners for gainful post-confinement careers, the manufacture of goods that would otherwise be produced offshore is inappropriate training. Furthermore, training in industries such as textiles and apparel, which already compete with low-cost imports, is of little value. A released inmate would find himself among the thousands of unemployed garment workers that would have lost their jobs to competition either from abroad or from within prisons.

Although there are flaws in the current status of prison labor initiatives and the proposed reform bill, UNITE understands the legitimate argument for providing prisoners with training opportunities that enhance rehabilitation. We would, however, prefer reforms that make prison industries less predatory and still allow for constructive activities for prisoners.

> *"Training in industries such as textiles and apparel, which already compete with low-cost imports, is of little value [to the prisoner]."*

To that end, UNITE has endorsed the Federal Prison Industries Competition in Contracting Act of 1997, H.R. 2758, which was introduced by Congressmen Peter Hoekstra and Barney Frank, Congresswoman Carolyn Maloney and more than 20 other members. We believe this bill strikes the appropriate balance between the need to keep prisoners employed and the need to maintain private sector employment.

This alternate bill contains several improvements over the bill that is currently being considered by this committee. For example, it would finally require Federal Prison Industries to compete for its contracts by eliminating the mandatory-source status of federal procurement. Under this improvement, the American taxpayer would no longer be forced to pay for over-priced or lesser-quality goods from prisons when a better option is available through the free market. The alternative bill would also enhance the opportunity for public participation in the FPI decision-making process.

UNITE strongly supports enhanced training programs within prisons, as long as prison labor programs are not destroying American jobs. If production of goods must continue as an element of prison industries, we believe such production should be only of those products for which there is no commercial market. Such prison labor initiatives would fulfill three valuable ends: prisoners would receive training; important goods, which are not commercially viable, would be produced; and law-abiding Americans would no longer face unfair and predatory competition from prison labor initiatives.

Prison Labor
Is Slave Labor

by John L. Zalusky

About the author: *John L. Zalusky is head of the Office of Wages and Industrial Relations of the Department of Economic Research of the American Federation of Labor and Congress of Industrial Organizations (AFL-CIO).*

Over the last two decades there have been numerous proposals to have convicts work at private-sector businesses before release, even to lease convicts to private-sector employers. This is not a new idea. In fact, it revisits one of the most corrupt, shameful, and repugnant periods of America's past.

For nearly 200 years, prisons were state-government profit centers that made more money than they cost to operate. Greed led to abuses and the abuses to universal revulsion. The corruption of business and state officials was only part of the problem. Convicts were forced to work, which led some prisoners to maim themselves to avoid hard and punishing labor. There were examples of convicts who were good workers getting extended sentences for minor infractions and poor workers getting out early. Conditions contributed to the federal government's building its own prison system to avoid housing its convicts in state prisons or city jails.

Nevertheless, many states continued to employ convicts through the 1930s, putting many firms out of business. The entire domestic wicker-furniture business was destroyed by prison factories in Illinois, Indiana, and Pennsylvania. The Minnesota prison system was in direct competition with International Harvester, John Deere, and other farm-implement firms.

The abuse of convicts by the various states was not unique. Worldwide revulsion led the International Labor Organization, a branch of the United Nations, to adopt conventions banning forced or compulsory labor. The United States followed suit and prohibited importation of convict-made goods.

The new generation of convict-labor advocates articulates two arguments. One is to cut the high cost of keeping convicts in prison. The other is to rehabilitate prisoners to reduce recidivism. The arguments don't hold up. Yet, it is necessary that convicts be kept busy all day, every day. Work is an important part of this activity and essential to convict control, which is the number one concern.

Employing convict labor is not a small risk for free American workers. It is a huge work force and is growing. There are now more than 1.5 million people in American prisons and jails. In 1993 there were nearly a million inmates in state prisons. As of December 1995, there are over 100,000 in the federal system, with the rest being local prisoners. This represents the highest incarceration rate in the world. In 1993, one of every 189 U.S. residents was in prison, three times as many as in 1980.

The impact of only half of these convicts taking free-labor jobs is equal to putting the entire employed civilian labor forces of Delaware and Rhode Island on the dole.

Although the nation's crime rate has been declining, the prison population has increased at six times our population growth rate. It is increasing because of mandatory sentences, parole limitations, and a variety of shortsighted get-tough policies.

A large share of those now behind bars are not U.S. citizens. The United States deported 50,000 illegal aliens in 1994. They were all in jail before they were deported, and many of them were taking jobs from U.S. workers. Ironically, these alien prisoners may be employed by the state to take a private-sector worker's job, while a private-sector employer would be fined for employing the same worker.

Does the Taxpayer Save Money?

To find savings in convict labor, the books have to be cooked. It costs between $15,000 and $22,000 per year to incarcerate a convict. However, each private-sector job contributes $50,000 to the economy. That's poor economics. Swapping a small saving in the cost of incarceration for a private-sector worker's job is poor economics.

Some states avoided the political and economic fallout by designing their prison industries to affect neighboring states rather than their own. For example, the high-quality, prison-made Minnesota Farm Implements sold cheaply in Minnesota. But the jobs lost were in Iowa, Wisconsin, and Illinois.

"Some convicts are now employed by private business cutting sugarcane in south Florida. Making convicts do this work could not be seen as rehabilitative."

Make no mistake; it is important that convicts work. The issue is really what they do and for whom. If convicts are not actively engaged, correctional officers are at risk. The riots and killings of Attica, New York, in the 1970s and Lucasville, Ohio, in 1993 are ever on the minds of correctional officers.

However, control of convicts is vital. Security limits the kind of rehabilitative work convicts can do and where it can be done. Care must be taken to prevent contraband from coming and going, weapons being made, or new crimes being committed. A significant share of prison riots have started in prison industries.

Is It Really Rehabilitative?

One program does not fit all, and the rehabilitation needs of convicts vary throughout the prison population. Many convicts had good jobs before they went to prison: There are doctors, lawyers, and a few politicians in prison. Some convicts are now employed by private business cutting sugarcane in south Florida. Making convicts do this work could not be seen as rehabilitative; it should be seen as added punishment.

Prisons have a reward/control/progression system that mitigates what few rehabilitation opportunities there are in a work program. When convicts arrive in prison, they are assigned to housekeeping chores that pay little or nothing. If a convict behaves and an opening occurs, he will be assigned to other work that is more challenging and pays a little more. It can take years for a convict to move up to the better-paying prison industry jobs. The convicts want this work badly because the alternative is to have nothing and do nothing.

Federal law now requires that federal convicts work. Twenty states have similar laws, and other states achieve the same result by regulations and rules. The 13th Amendment abolished slavery except for convicts. To dispel doubt about what we are talking about, Black's Law Dictionary defines a slave as "a person who is wholly subject to the will of another; one who has no freedom of action, but whose person and services are wholly under the control of another."

The issue is not whether convicts work. What is being suggested by [former Delaware governor] Pete du Pont, [Senator] Phil Gramm, and a few others is a slave work force, without labor standards and under contract to private business, which will take work from other businesses that use free labor and pay free-market wages.

There are things convicts can do with their time that facilitate their control and rehabilitation and do not threaten private-sector jobs. Convicts can still improve their educational qualifications for future employment. However, earlier get-tough moves took away the incentive for educational achievement, such as GEDs, and the new Republican majority in Congress took Pell Grants away from convicts in 1995.

> *"What is being suggested . . . is a slave work force, without labor standards and under contract to private business, which will take work from other businesses."*

This, of course, increased the risk to prison security forces, increased sentences and the size of the prison population, and decreased really effective rehabilitation programs. These measures have done a lot to frustrate effective rehabilitation through training and education.

The Walsh-Healy Government Contracts Act of 1936 prohibits the federal government from buying convict-made goods except those made by federal prison industries. UNICOR, an independent federal corporation with a representative board of directors, polices this system. In short, goods made in federal prisons by convicts are made for the federal government (the self-use principle). The federal system with UNICOR has been completely free of corruption, something that cannot be said of the state systems.

In the 1920s, nearly half of the prison population was forced to work. Many states used convict labor before the 1930s, sometimes leasing it to a few private businesses and in other cases forming their own state corporations. But cheap convict labor became the basis of unfair competition in many private businesses, large and small. The reaction was a 40-year ban on the interstate shipment of goods mined or manufactured with the use of convicts.

In 1979, the Ashurst-Sumner Act was amended, allowing for seven prison industry enhancement (PIE) programs. Subsequent amendments followed, and now all 50 states and their county and city jails can have PIE programs. PIE is a euphemism for private industry using convict labor and being able to ship products in interstate and international commerce.

To have a PIE program, a state must promise the federal Bureau of Justice Assistance that convicts will be paid locally prevailing wages, that the state will advise local labor (generally nothing more than a letter), and that prison labor will have no adverse impact on local employment. The Eighth Circuit Court of Appeals found in 1994 that the Ashurst-Sumner Act is designed to protect "private businesses," and convicts have no private right to claim wages under the law. In 15 years, the bureau has never brought an enforcement action against a state for failing to abide by these simple standards, and there have been numerous published examples of violations.

Some states are taking advantage of the PIE programs, using slave labor and taking jobs from the private sector. Some examples: Arizona convicts are now working on new Shelby Cobra sports cars, building limousines, and manufacturing electrical fixtures. This is work many free workers would like to have, not at slave wages but at free-market wages. The same is true of the convicts making Prison Blues jeans in the Oregon state prison system. In short, there is work being done in prisons that private-sector workers want at a fair wage. This situation is what du Pont, Gramm, and other conservatives want to expand.

Turning convicts over to private-sector employers without regard to market wages and benefits or the freedom to leave the workplace would revisit a shameful part of U.S. history. It would use convicts as slaves, make paupers of free labor, and bankrupt some businesses while benefiting a favored few. The whole idea is an affront to free-world standards and adds risk to the job of correctional officers.

Prison Labor May Pose a Threat to Public Safety

by Christine Long-Wagner

About the author: *Christine Long-Wagner is a contributor to* Shield, *the magazine of the Law Enforcement Alliance of America.*

Have I got a wake-up call for you!

What would you say if you knew that prison inmates might have access to such private information as medical records? You might ask, "How do they get access to all of that information?" What would you say if I responded, "It's a part of the job!"

In case you missed the *Prime Time Live* episode that aired on October 22, 1997, I feel a responsibility to pass this information on to you.

One of their stories concerned inmates in some of our prisons and detention centers and the various jobs they hold. Chris Wallace was the chief correspondent for this story. Let me fill you in on some of the highlights from the show that evening.

The program started out with a felon, previously convicted of burglary, forgery, and theft, who was working with a group of inmates doing telemarketing from inside a Utah State Prison. He was taking down information such as names, addresses, and any references he could get from the people that he called.

In Iowa, the state's "800" tourism line rang directly into a maximum security prison where inmates would not only find out where the caller lived, but also when they would be away from home.

Booking Your TWA Reservations from Prisons

Have you traveled by TWA lately? Did you have any idea that a criminal from a youth detention center in Ventura, California, might possibly be the one handling your travel arrangements? I was told by a corrections officer that when an inmate makes a call out of a prison in California, there is a recording that periodically states that the call is coming from a prison. Ultimately, however, there is no such recording for you or me telling us that we have dialed into a prison to make our plane reservations.

One inmate, a convicted thief who had been working as a telemarketing agent, was caught after his release using someone else's credit card number, a number that he had picked up as part of his employment while in the prison. Apparently, he went on a spending spree that totaled over $15,000. When he was caught, he had in his possession more than 60 other credit card numbers that had been stolen from other TWA customers. Naturally, TWA was not willing to be interviewed.

> *"Did you have any idea that a criminal from a youth detention center in Ventura, California, might possibly be the one handling your travel arrangements?"*

Sandstar Family Entertainment, a company that employs inmates from Utah, was willing to be interviewed for the TV program. The spokesperson for this company said that they instruct these criminals not to tell people that they are calling from a prison. He actually said that information that the caller is a convict currently serving time in prison is not pertinent to the consumer!

Apparently, the problem is not limited to just Utah, California and Iowa. In Washington state, the Red Cross is using prison inmates for fundraising-related work. There are 33 states participating in programs such as the ones mentioned above.

In Texas, prisoners were processing car titles. The titles were smuggled out to accomplices who would steal cars that closely matched the make and model on the stolen titles. A prison industry supervisor and a corrections officer were involved in this ring. Although inmates no longer perform this work at the Texas prisons, they do process documents for government agencies such as tax information, patient medical files, and court rulings.

The supporters of these programs claim that using convicts to process all this information has saved taxpayers three million dollars. No one seems too concerned about the information this puts at the inmates' fingertips and given their propensity to commit crime (after all, they had to commit some offense to be in prison in the first place), what they might do with it.

And that is not the end of the problem. I am sure many of you are familiar with the consumer surveys that many of us have filled out and mailed away in return for free coupons and free samples. Some of the information asked for on these types of surveys include address, whether or not you are married, how much money you make per year, what type of appliances you have, what make of car you drive, what camera equipment you use, etc.! On this segment of *Prime Time Live*, it was shown how the results of a customer survey, sent out by a company named Metromail, were processed by criminals in prison. Of course, Metromail didn't want to speak on camera—and I can understand why.

Prison Information Exchange

In this particular case a grandmother from Ohio received a handwritten, twelve-page, sexually explicit letter from a convicted rapist in a Huntsville, Texas, prison. He told her about his sexual fantasies involving her and he said he wanted to "visit" her. She is terrified! She sleeps with two pieces of metal pipe next to her bed. This inmate is going to be released within the next year. He admitted on camera that he got this woman's personal information from another inmate who obtained it from processing of the aforementioned surveys. This convicted rapist bought the information for twenty-five cents!

Why is all this happening? Plain and simple: the priority here is profit. Given that inmates provide cheap and easy labor, and with the proliferation of private prisons which are run for profit rather than for public safety/punishment, the trend will likely only increase. Some prison administrators claim that the purpose of providing this type of employment to inmates is to teach them a trade, but I would have to argue that giving inmates work which allows them access to personal information or to information that helps them continue to commit new crimes is going too far!

It's more like helping them perfect their criminal trade rather than teaching a legitimate job skill! Perhaps the people running these prisons have forgotten what the purpose of our prison system is supposed to be: to punish the convicted and to protect the public from the same.

> *"One inmate, a convicted thief . . . was caught after his release using someone else's credit card number, a number that he had picked up as part of his employment while in prison."*

The goal should not be to make more of a profit for themselves or for some other corporation.

At the end of the program several comments were made: TWA is still using prison inmates despite the problem they ran into with the convicted thief; Metromail says they no longer use prison labor after what happened with the grandmother from Ohio; and Sandstar Family Entertainment no longer lets inmates see the public's addresses.

Seeking a Legislative Solution

I am certain you would agree that these are meager efforts, hardly enough to correct what has been a very serious—albeit not very well known—problem. During the past LEAA Board Meeting, we watched the *Prime Time Live* tape and it led to much discussion. We are trying to decide exactly how we, as an organization, should proceed to stop this kind of prison profiteering practice. The first step must be public education and the second is to make your voice heard.

In order to do so, I urge you to write or call your state and federal representatives, to let them know that you are strongly against the practice of allowing prison inmates to handle any private information in any way, shape or form. Be on the lookout for more examples of this kind of abuse and be wary of the push to transform our prisons into greed-driven, profit-generating businesses.

And as always, be careful with the private information you give out—especially over the phone. Remember, no one can look out for your security better than you.

Bibliography

Books

David C. Anderson   *Sensible Justice.* New York: New Press, 1998.

Joe Arpaio and   *America's Toughest Sheriff: How We Can Win the War Against*
Len Sherman   *Crime.* Arlington, TX: Summit, 1996.

Daniel Burton-Rose,   *The Celling of America: An Inside Look at the U.S. Prison*
Dan Pens, and   *Industry.* Monroe, ME: Common Courage Press, 1998.
Paul Wright, eds.

Jean Marie Christenson   *The Keepers and the Caged: Heroes and Necromancers in the*
                           Prison System Today. Dubuque, IA: Kendall/Hunt, 1996.

Elliott Currie   *Crime and Punishment in America.* New York: Henry Holt,
                           1998.

Pete Earley   *The Hot House: Life Inside Leavenworth Prison.* New York:
                           Bantam Books, 1995.

Kenneth C. Haas and   *The Dilemmas of Corrections: Contemporary Readings.*
Geoffrey P. Alpert, eds.   Prospect Heights, IL: Waveland Press, 1998.

Richard Harding   *Private Prisons and Public Accountability.* Piscataway, NJ:
                           Transaction, 1997.

Adrian L. James,   *Privatizing Prisons: Rhetoric and Reality.* Newbury Park, CA:
A. Keith Bottomley,   Sage, 1997.
Alison Liebling,
and Emma Clare

Robert Johnson   *Hard Time: Understanding and Reforming the Prison.*
                           Belmont, CA: Wadsworth, 1995.

Kenneth Kerle   *American Jails: Looking to the Future.* Woburn, MA:
                           Butterworth/Heinemann, 1998.

Elihu Rosenblatt   *Criminal Injustice: Confronting the Prison Crisis.* Cambridge,
                           MA: South End Press, 1996.

David Shichor   *Punishment for Profit: Private Prisons/Public Concerns.*
                           Newbury Park, CA: Sage, 1995.

Bibliography

Glenn D. Walters   *Changing Lives of Crime and Drugs: Intervening with Substance-Abusing Offenders.* New York: John Wiley & Sons, 1998.

Franklin E. Zimring and Gordon Hawkins   *Incapacitation: Penal Confinement and the Restraint of Crime.* New York: Oxford University Press, 1995.

Periodicals

Stephen Belenko and Jordan Peugh   "Fighting Crime by Treating Substance Abuse," *Issues in Science and Technology,* Fall 1998.

Warren Cohen   "Need Work? Go to Jail," *U.S. News & World Report,* December 9, 1996.

Pete du Pont   "Should Prisoners Work?" *World & I,* March 1, 1996. Available from *The World & I,* 3400 New York Ave. NE, Washington, DC 20002.

David L. Evans   "Lost Behind Prison Bars," *Newsweek,* September 7, 1998.

Karin Fischer   "Is Locking 'em Up the Answer?" *Washington Monthly,* January/February 1998.

Russ Freyman   "Jails in a Jam," *Governing,* March 1998.

Stephen Fuchs   "Justice for Our Time," *World & I,* June 1, 1996.

Jessica Gavora   "The Prisoner's Accomplice," *Policy Review,* September/October 1996.

Nick Gillespie   "Prisoners' Dilemma: Private Jails Are Easier to Reform," *Reason,* November 1997.

Spencer P.M. Harrington   "Caging the Crazy: 'Supermax' Confinement Under Attack," *Humanist,* January 11, 1997.

Sam Hine   "The Prison Boom: Corporate Profits, Human Losses," *Witness,* November 1998.

John Linton   "Inmate Education Makes Sense," *Corrections Today,* June 1998. Available from the American Correctional Association Inc., 4380 Forbes Blvd., Lanham, MD 20706-4322.

Joe Loconte   "Jailhouse Rock of Ages," *Policy Review,* July/August 1997.

Jerome Miller   "Can We Break Free of a Failed Criminal-Justice System?" *U.S. Catholic,* June 1996.

John J. Rafferty   "Prison Industry: The Next Step," *Corrections Today,* July 1998.

Woody West   "Resurrected Chain Gangs Link Crime to Punishment," *Insight on the News,* June 12, 1995. Available from News World Communications, Inc., 3600 New York Ave. N.E., Washington, DC 20002.

Daniel B. Wood   "Private Prisons, Public Doubts," *Christian Science Monitor,* July 21, 1998.

Robert Worth   "A Model Prison," *Atlantic Monthly,* November 1995.

Organizations to Contact

The editors have compiled the following list of organizations concerned with the issues debated in this book. The descriptions are derived from materials provided by the organizations. All have publications or information available for interested readers. The list was compiled on the date of publication of the present volume; the information provided here may change. Be aware that many organizations take several weeks or longer to respond to inquiries, so allow as much time as possible.

American Civil Liberties Union (ACLU)
National Prison Project
1875 Connecticut Ave. NW, Suite 410, Washington, DC 20009
(202) 234-4830 • fax: (202) 234-4890
e-mail: aclu@aclu.org • website: http://www.aclu.org

Formed in 1972, the project serves as a national resource center and litigates cases to strengthen and protect adult and juvenile offenders' Eighth Amendment rights. It opposes electronic monitoring of offenders and the privatization of prisons. The project publishes the quarterly *National Prison Project Journal* and various booklets.

American Correctional Association (ACA)
4380 Forbes Blvd., Lanham, MD 20706-4322
(800) 222-5646 • (301) 918-1800 • fax: (301) 918-1900
e-mail: harryw@aca.org • website: http://www.corrections.com/aca

ACA is committed to improving national and international correctional policy and to promoting the professional development of those working in the field of corrections. It offers a variety of books and correspondence courses on corrections and criminal justice and publishes the bimonthly magazine *Corrections Today*.

Amnesty International (AI)
322 Eighth Ave., New York, NY 10001
(212) 807-8400 • fax: (212) 627-1451
website: http://www.amnesty-usa.org

Amnesty International is an independent worldwide movement working impartially for the release of all prisoners of conscience, fair and prompt trials for political prisoners, and an end to torture and executions. AI is funded by donations from its members and supporters throughout the world. The organization publishes books, reports, and the bimonthly *Amnesty International Newsletter*.

Campaign for an Effective Crime Policy
918 F St. NW, Suite 505, Washington, DC 20004
(202) 628-1903 • fax: (202) 628-1091
e-mail: info@crimepolicy.com • website: http://www.sproject.com/cecp.htm

Launched in 1992 by a group of criminal justice leaders, the nonpartisan Campaign for an Effective Crime Policy advocates alternative sentencing policies. It also works to educate the public about the relative effectiveness of various strategies for improving public safety. The campaign has published a series of reports on issues in criminal justice, including "'Three Strikes' Laws: Five Years Later."

Cato Institute
1000 Massachusetts Ave. NW, Washington, DC 20001-5403
(202) 842-0200 • fax: (202) 842-3490
e-mail: cato@cato.org • website: http://www.cato.org

The institute is a libertarian public policy research foundation dedicated to limiting the role of government and protecting individual liberties. The institute evaluates government policies and offers reform proposals in its publication *Policy Analysis.* Topics include "Prison Blues: How America's Foolish Sentencing Policies Endanger Public Safety" and "Crime, Police, and Root Causes." In addition, the institute publishes the quarterly magazine *Regulation*, the bimonthly *Cato Policy Report*, and numerous books.

Center for Alternative Sentencing and Employment Services (CASES)
346 Broadway, 8th Fl., New York, NY 10013
(212) 732-0076 • fax: (212) 571-0292
e-mail: careym@cases.org • website: http://www.cases.org/education/cases

CASES seeks to end what it views as the overuse of incarceration as a response to crime. It operates two alternative-sentencing programs in New York City: the Court Employment Project, which provides intensive supervision and services for felony offenders, and the Community Service Sentencing Project, which works with repeat misdemeanor offenders. The center advocates in court for such offenders' admission into its programs. CASES publishes various program brochures.

Families Against Mandatory Minimums (FAMM)
1612 K St. NW, Suite 1400, Washington, DC 20006
(202) 822-6700 • fax: (202) 822-6704
e-mail: famm@famm.org • website: http://www.famm.org

FAMM is an educational organization that works to repeal mandatory minimum sentences. It provides legislators, the public, and the media with information on and analyses of minimum-sentencing laws. FAMM publishes the quarterly newsletter *FAMM-gram.*

The Heritage Foundation
214 Massachusetts Ave. NE, Washington, DC 20002
(202) 546-4400 • fax: (202) 546-8328
e-mail: pubs@heritage.org • http://www.heritage.org

The Heritage Foundation is a conservative public policy research institute. It is a proponent of limited government and advocates tougher sentencing and the construction of more prisons. The foundation publishes articles on a variety of public policy issues in its Backgrounder series and in its quarterly journal *Policy Review.*

John Howard Society (JHS)
771 Montreal St., Kingston, ON, K7K 3J6 CANADA
(613) 542-7547 • fax: (613) 542-6824
e-mail: national@johnhoward.ca • website: http://www.johnhoward.ca

The John Howard Society of Canada advocates reform in the criminal justice system and monitors governmental policy to ensure fair and compassionate treatment of prisoners. It views imprisonment as a last resort option. The organization provides education to the community, support services to at-risk youth, and rehabilitation programs to former inmates. Its publications include the booklet *Literacy and the Courts: Protecting the Right to Understand.*

Law Enforcement Alliance of America (LEAA)
7700 Leesburg Pike, Ste. 421, Falls Church, VA 20043
(800) 766-8578 • fax: (703) 556-6485
webstie: http://www.leaa.org

Comprising more than sixty-five thousand members and supporters, the Law Enforcement Alliance of America is the nation's largest coalition of law enforcement professionals, victims of crime, and concerned citizens dedicated to making America safer. It publishes the quarterly journal *The Shield.*

National Center for Policy Analysis (NCPA)
655 15th St. NW, Suite 375, Washington, DC 20005
(202) 628-6671 • fax: (202) 628-6474
e-mail: ncpa@public-policy.org • website: http://www.ncpa.org

NCPA is a nonprofit public policy research institute. It advocates more stringent prison sentences, the abolishment of parole, and restitution for crimes. Publications include the policy reports "Why Expected Punishment Deters Crime," "Parolees Return to Crime," and "Restitution Works for Juveniles."

National Center on Institutions and Alternatives (NCIA)
635 Slaters Lane, Suite G-100, Alexandria, VA 222314
(703) 684-0373 • fax: (703) 684-6037
website: http://www.ncianet.org/ncia

NCIA is a criminal justice foundation that encourages community-based alternatives to prison that are more effective in providing education, training, and personal skills required for the rehabilitation of nonviolent offenders. The center advocates doubling "good conduct" credit for the early release of nonviolent first-time offenders in the federal system to make room for violent offenders. NCIA publishes books, reports, and the periodic newsletters *Criminal Defense Update* and *Jail Suicide/Mental Health Update.*

National Crime Prevention Council (NCPC)
1700 K St. NW, 2nd Fl., Washington, DC 20006-3817
(202) 261-4111 • fax: (202) 296-1356
e-mail: webmaster@ncpc.org • website: http://www.ncpc.org

The NCPC provides training and technical assistance to groups and individuals interested in crime prevention. It advocates job training and recreation programs as a means to reduce crime and violence. The council, which sponsors the Take a Bite Out of Crime campaign, publishes the newsletter *Catalyst*, which is published ten times a year.

Police Foundation (PF)
1201 Connecticut Ave. NW, Washington, DC 20036
(202) 833-1460 • fax: (202) 659-9149
e-mail: pfinfo@policefoundation.org • website: http://www.policefoundation.org

The Police Foundation is committed to increasing police effectiveness in controlling crime, maintaining order, and providing humane and efficient service. The foundation sponsors forums that debate and disseminate ideas to improve personnel and practice in American criminal policing. It publishes a number of books, reports, and handbooks regarding all aspects of the criminal justice system.

Prison Fellowship Ministries (PFM)
PO Box 17500, Washington, DC 20041-0500
(703) 478-0100
website: http://www.prisonfellowship.org

Prison Fellowship Ministries encourages Christians to work in prisons and to assist communities in ministering to prisoners, ex-offenders, and their families. It works toward establishing a fair and effective criminal justice system and trains volunteers for in-prison ministries. Publications include the monthly *Jubilee* newsletter, the quarterly *Justice Report*, and numerous books, including *Born Again* and *Life Sentence*.

The Sentencing Project
918 F St. NW, Suite 501, Washington, DC 20004
(202) 628-0871 • fax: (202) 628-1091
e-mail: staff@sentencingproject.org • website: http://www.sentencingproject.org

The project seeks to provide public defenders and other public officials with information on establishing and improving alternative sentencing programs that provide convicted persons with positive and constructive options to incarceration. It promotes increased public understanding of the sentencing process and alternative sentencing programs. It publishes the reports "Americans Behind Bars: A Comparison of International Rates of Incarceration" and "Young Black Men and the Criminal Justice System: A Growing National Problem."

U.S. Department of Justice
Federal Bureau of Prisons
320 First St. NW, Washington, DC 20534
e-mail: webmaster@bop.gov • website: http://www.bop.gov

The Federal Bureau of Prisons works to protect society by confining offenders in the controlled environments of prisons and community-based facilities. It believes in providing work and other self-improvement opportunities within these facilities to assist offenders in becoming law-abiding citizens. The bureau publishes the book *The State of the Bureau*.

Index

Index